A Sc

THE STORY OF EIGHT GENERATIONS

Published by

Librario Publishing Ltd

ISBN: 1-904440-51-7

Copies can be ordered via the Internet
www.librario.com

or from:

Brough House, Milton Brodie, Kinloss
Moray IV36 2UA
Tel /Fax No 00 44 (0)1343 850 617

Printed and bound by Digisource GB Ltd

A Scottish Family

The Story of Eight Generations

Betty Willsher

Librario

Previous publications by the Author

School Before Five	1959	Faber and Faber Ltd
Tales of Professor Popoff	1961	Pergamon Press
The Flying Jacket	1964	Blackie and Son
Call Me Person	1969	Pergamon Press
Stones (with Doreen Hunter)	1978	Canongate
Understanding Scottish Gravestones	1985	W & R Chambers & CSA (reprinted Canongate Books)
How to Record Scottish Graveyards	1985	CSA
Scottish Epitaphs	1996	Canongate Books
St Andrews – Ancient City in the Twentieth Century	2003	Librario
St Andrews Citizens – Their Societies, Past and Present	2003	Librario

To My Family, past, present and future

ACKNOWLEDGEMENTS

I would like to thank all those who have helped me compile this book. First I owe much to my daughter Penny Walker, to my sister Maryan Huntridge and brother John Anderson, to my New Zealand cousins John and Shirley Russell, Vivienne and Jack McLean and Ruth and Michael Buckenham; to my Elgin cousins Dorothy Adam and Anne and Sandy Adam. I am grateful for information from Rob and Jean Bartholomew, Edinburgh, Dorothy and Stewart Wallace in Savannah, USA, Anne Wescott in the Yukon, Canada, and Mary Laanela, Victoria Island, BC. My family has given me a wide range of photographs from which to choose and I thank them; also *The Northern Scot* and Brian Donaldson for illustration. I would acknowledge the most helpful services of the Archivist Department at Aberdeen Library, and those of Mrs Heron, Local Heritage Department, Elgin Library.

CONTENTS

PREFACE

This is the story of eight generations of a Scottish family. By chance the oldest child in the family has been a daughter. It is set in Elgin, Peebles, Edinburgh, St Andrews, London and County Durham. I was fortunate in that I inherited from my mother diaries and letters of my grandmother and letters of her father, which she had kept. There was also a good deal of relevant material in the archives at Elgin.

My search began when I retired. I started to go to East Register House on Mondays, with a research student at St Andrews. He had come from his home in South America, partly to trace his Scottish ancestors. We were fortunate; it was at the time when we were able to study the Old Parish Registers – in the flesh – not on film or microfiche. I remember one visit when I was looking up records for a family (on my father's Anderson side) called Husband. Robert and I had both worked hard all day. When we boarded the train to go home, we settled at a table for four. "Well, how did you get on today?" I asked Robert. "Fine," he replied, "I had three lovely deaths. What about you?" I was a bit dispirited, and replied, "I'm still looking for a Husband". The man opposite me looked horrified, gathered up his brief case and retreated to settle at another table.

There are certainly ups and downs in the game. Oh, the joys when a link is found, the setbacks when one draws a blank, the satisfactions on drawing up family trees on paper! But there is more to it than that. Holidays become searches for houses where one's ancestors lived or graves where they rest. Visits to already-known cousins and to newly discovered cousins are meaningful and exciting. I went to the United States and to Canada, and, most heart-warming of all, to New Zealand. My mother's cousin Eden Russell and his son John met me at the airport at Christchurch, and we went to stay with Eden and

Eileen in Dunedin. We had a drinks' tray at hand and the charts set out on a large table. We worked on them with great enthusiasm. Then we went to Queenstown, and after that to Lake Hayes to stay with John's sister Vivienne, her husband and their children. Later I stayed with the two families at Invercargill. There were picnics and barbecues with their sister Ruth and family. There were sailings and outings. Best of all they have come to Scotland on visits, and we all share a special love of Elgin and our Elgin cousins.

I was worried lest I set back the readers of this book by giving detailed family trees, so I have narrowed the spread and given abbreviated charts relating to this book. I hope I may be forgiven by my relatives if I have omitted some co-lateral branches of the family.

The changes in lives of women between 1800 and the present day are evident in this family story; in the early days no lady councillors, no university degrees, few small families, but plenty of help in the house. And after generations of most of the families living in the same area, their descendants are scattered over the world.

I have found that in writing this book I have begun to appreciate and to care more deeply for my grandparents, my parents – and others who have died – than ever before.

Betty Willsher

LIST OF ILLUSTRATIONS

CHAPTER 1

JOHN RUSSEL AND JANET RUSSELL

John Russel, my great-great-grandfather, was the son of a farmer in Cloves in the parish of Alves, Morayshire. There were several Russell families on farms in Alves parish; this one was a branch of the Carden Russels. John set up as a merchant and flourished. His shop was in Elgin High Street, and when the Assembly Rooms were built in 1822, he moved his business to the arcades on the ground floor. (Regrettably the Assembly Rooms were demolished in 1969 to make way for the building of the Royal Bank). I have copies of unpaid accounts made out in John's own handwriting; they show he dealt in tweed and other materials, in gloves and hats, ribbons and such. His portrait shows that he was fair, with a long oval face, blue eyes, a rather prominent nose and a small but full-lipped mouth. In 1805 he was 35 years old and unmarried. He was a member of the Elgin Merchant Guildry and its treasurer for seventeen years.

Bailie John Russel of Elgin, from a portrait

In early September 1805 John set out on horseback to visit the Borders. The travels of another member of the Guildry, Isaac Forsyth, may well have given John the idea of a similar journey. Isaac Forsyth was a bookseller and owner of the first lending library in Scotland; his business was carried out in the remarkable old house, The Tower, which still stands by the Plainstones on the north side of Elgin High Street. In 1779 Isaac and a friend set off from Elgin on horseback. They were on their way for twenty-five days, riding five hundred and sixty-six miles, and in the last day covering forty-two miles.

John Russel's journey was less ambitious. His aim was to visit the new mills at Galashiels and possibly make some business transactions. He went on to spend a few days in Peebles and there visited a family with the same name as himself. This Russell family lived in School Brae, and I found information about them in the Memoirs of Robert Chambers.

> The Minister's chief elder in my early days was a cart and millwright, a substantial citizen, related by marriage to our family, and with whose domestic life I was consequently well acquainted. Language fails me in expressing my sense of the goodness and worth of this old man, though from the narrowness of his sphere of life he had never learned to temper his piety with any share of liberality. He afforded a perfect example of the religious practice of a former age, and would have been considered rather stern by the bulk of his contemporaries. Tammas, as he was familiarly called, had a large family of sons and daughters whom he governed with relentless austerity. Any approach to gaiety of spirits was deemed highly improper, and dancing was positively sinful.

Robert Chambers then recounts this incident.

> I could forgive anything in Tammas but the sternness. In the hands of his kind Christianity did not appear as a religion of love: it seemed almost wholly to consist of an imposition of irksome duties and an abstinence from all natural and allowable enjoyments. A company of strolling players came to Peebles to negotiate for permission to use the town hall as a theatre. When the suppliant approached, Tammas was hewing a log out of doors, and stood with his axe suspended over his head while listening to the request.
>
> "I'll oppose it with all the means in my poo'ers, sir," he said.
>
> "Not with the hatchet I hope, sir," responded the son of Thespis.
>
> The poor man had to set up his scenes in the upper room of a public house – thither my brother and were taken to see our first play *Inkle and Yarico*.

16

('Tammas' was certainly behind the times. In 1784 when Mrs Siddons was playing in Edinburgh, the General Assembly altered its timetable to allow delegates to attend the matinee.)

Thomas Russell had inherited from his father, Alexander Russell, the house, the workshop and the rigg at the top and east side of School Brae, which runs from the High Street to Tweed Green. His father Alexander has been to me a mystery man, a real problem in my family search. Two clues were given in the family papers of my mother and her mother. One was that this Alexander was a son of the youngest son of William Russell of Ashiestiel; the other that he had inherited lands at Stobo, but had forfeited them for his part in the 1745 rebellion. If this was relayed to Thomas Russell he never disclosed it.

When John made his first visit to Peebles in 1805, he must have been struck by its serene beauty. Chambers wrote: "Peebles was little advanced from the condition it had mainly rested in for several hundred years." And Cockburn remarked of it: "Peebles is as quiet as the grave." He also recounted that an inhabitant, who had been on a visit to Paris, said on his return, "Paris is a wonderful place, but still, it is Peebles for pleasure." Thomas put up at the Inn, and after he had seen to his horse, had a wash and taken his tea, he went for a stroll. He located School Brae; at that time the two schools were situated at the bottom of School Brae. There were some features in common with Elgin. The Tweed was if anything broader than the Lossie, yet each was a fine sight. Tweed Green put him in mind of the Green north of Elgin High Street where the wifies and the lassies laid out their washing to dry.

When John called at the Russell house he was pleased that he was given a warm welcome. Thomas and his wife Margaret Grieve had a family of ten children; only one had been lost in early childhood. There were two sons, Alexander (Sandy) who was with his father in the business, and David who, with his three younger sisters, was still at school. The two eldest girls were wed, but John was introduced to Elizabeth and Janet, and was impressed by their demeanour and their pretty faces.

David Grieve of Jedderfield, Peebles, painted miniature

Mrs Russell was the fifth child of David Grieve, a farmer at Jedderfield (he had died eight years ago). On the second day of John's visit she and the two daughters took John for a walk up to her old home. Jedderfield stands high on the crag beside Neidpath Castle. Today you will find it above the golf course, the old house long since converted into barns and a new house built. From here you look down and see the whole of Peebles, which lies in a basin, and the broad river Tweed flowing on its course. David Grieve was described in Chambers' Memoirs as a well-known agriculturalist. When the army was advancing in 1745 the folk of Peebles were in fear and locked their doors. But "a farmer in the neighbourhood of the town having displayed a discreet desire to accommodate them, by killing two pet lambs, and causing his wife and servant to bake oatmeal cakes for them all … was treated with great politeness and had his poultry and cattle scrupulously spared."

Margaret Russell spoke well of her father, of her happy childhood at Jedderfield and of how her children loved their visits to their grandparents. John Russel shared with her the love of a peaceful county life. When the time came for John to leave for Elgin he found it hard to go. Something had happened to him, something unforeseen. Being a cautious man, when he got home he thought things over with great care. Eventually he wrote a letter to Thomas Russell, to ask for the hand of his daughter Janet! He gave his full credentials: his financial standing, the fact that he was an elder in the kirk, a member of the Merchant Guildry, and so forth. Thomas considered it was a good offer and accepted it. We know nothing of Janet's feelings. The marriage was arranged for a year hence, and took place on 17 September 1806 in the drawing room of the manse, with the Reverend William Dalgleish officiating. Deacon Chambers was a witness. John may have worn a blue broadcloth suit and the young bride a dress of cream silk in the style of the day, with a very high waist, her hair in curls at the front and a roll on top with a high comb. Sadly there is no picture of her at any time of her life, only a shadow silhouette of John, and his portrait, which is in New Zealand now. For the important journey to Elgin John had bought a gig. The bride's trousseau – her clothes, her linen, and wedding gifts – had been packed in a large and very handsome gentlemen's wardrobe, which her father had made for her. It was taken by cart to Leith and from thence transported to Lossiemouth by ship, and again by cart to

Elgin. This piece of furniture was passed down the generations of our family until recently.

How did Janet feel as they drove north? She was just eighteen and Mr Russel must have seemed almost a stranger, and so very much older than herself. The only thing we know is that when she reached her new home in Elgin and unpacked her trousseau, she wept with loneliness and longing to be back with her own folk at Peebles. There were gifts to unwrap at Elgin – one of them a twelve-place set of Elgin silver cutlery with the initials JJR for John and Janet Russel. She kept a stout heart and did her best, and the loneliness was assuaged when her first child was born on 11 September 1807. He was named Thomas after Janet's father, and her parents and her Uncle Thomas Grieve came up to Elgin for the baptism.

As was almost inevitable in those days the family steadily increased; James was born in June 1809, which pleased the Cloves grandparents; John in July 1911 and then Alexander, from whom I am descended, on 27 January 1813. At last two girls were born, Margaret in August 1815 and Janet in July 1819, and then, to complete the family, Francis William Russell in 1822. He was named after the Provost, Francis William Grant. The baptismal entries – the choice of names, the spacing in dates of birth, and the names of the witnesses – make an interesting social document. The family was friendly with teachers, writers, businessmen. The surnames of the children are all given as Russell but John continued to sign his name Russel on documents.

The Russells were members of St Giles Church, an ancient building. There were lofts for the Guildry, the Weavers, the Glovers, the Magistrates and the Lairds, and galleries for the Earl of Fife, the Earl of Seafield and the Earl of Moray. Once a year, on the evening of the first Sunday in November, the church was lit up from the four chandeliers brilliant with candles, and from the candles of the master tradesmen, and those of many families, making five hundred candles in all. In 1826 there was need for repairs, and although the pillars and walls were "as strong as rocks" the decision was made to build a new church.

On 1 October a most moving sermon was preached by the Reverend Richard Rose. He took as his text "And David made him houses and prepared a place for the ark of God and pitched for it a tent". He referred to the solemn circumstances in which they were placed, that "in this ancient church, where their fathers had worshipped and taken sweet counsel for generations, the voice of the Gospel would be heard no more… It might have been spared at small expense, there being memories connected with it which no new building, however splendid, could produce or foster." However, no sooner had the congregation been dismissed than the contractor began to take down the slates from the roof and in the course of two months it was levelled to the ground. Some may have regretted the loss, but most admired the handsome new building, which was in the style of the Grecian temple of Lysacritis. This church, which holds a congregation of seventeen hundred, was opened for worship on 28 October 1828. The historic bell had been taken from the old kirk. In 1713 it had been rent by a woman striking it with a large key to raise the alarm because her house was on fire. When it was recast the citizens of Elgin threw in silver coins while the metal was smelting.

During the lifetime of Janet and John, fine buildings at the east and west end of the town were erected through the generosity of men who had been brought up in Elgin. In 1816 Dr Gray's Hospital was built at a cost of £6000 from a legacy of Dr Alexander Gray, and is still a boon to the citizens of Elgin today. Another donor to the town was General Alexander Anderson. When his young mother was widowed, it is said that she walked all the way from London to Elgin carrying her baby in her arms. Although her parents lived in the area, there had been a quarrel about her marriage. She went to the cathedral and cradled her baby in the font in the ruins. But she was so weak and so ill that she had to be helped and shortly died. The child, who came to have a prestigious army career, was given a home and was educated. In gratitude for this, General Anderson left a handsome legacy for the erection and maintenance of Anderson's Institution "For the support of

Old Age and Education of Youth". It offered homes for ten adults and for fifty destitute children, and a large and well-attended Free School and a School of Industry. This handsome classical building was opened in 1830. John Russel's son, Alexander, and his descendants almost to this day, have been involved in the running of Anderson's Institution.

During the nineteenth century the citizens of Elgin responded generously to numerous subscription lists. In 1801 through their gifts the English and the Grammar School were replaced by Elgin Academy. It was built round three sides of a quadrangle and comprised of an English School, a Classical School (commonly called the Latin School), and a Mathematical school. The master of each of these was autonomous. The Russell boys received a good education at the Academy.

Elgin was a fine place for children. There was little crime, and so plenty of freedom. There were regular entertainments on the days of fairs and the celebrations of Royal births and marriages. In 1836 Mr Wombwell's Royal National Menagerie visited Elgin. *The Courant* notice read:

> There are two elephants, the male the largest and most singular animal ever seen. There are seven lions which were bred in Glasgow; also Royal Bengal tigers and several leopards and leopardesses, three of them only six weeks old. They are to be seen being suckled by their mother, a very pleasing and most interesting sight. There are also hyenas, a sloth, a porcupine, a mandril, a pair of Alpaca hyenas, the wild ass of the scriptures, a variety of monkeys, and ostriches, pelicans and serpents, crocodiles and alligators.

One can imagine the excitement in the Russell household.

Janet and John saw heartening changes in their home town. It was not until 1822 that the streets were paved and pavements made. Provost Innes declared, "I have paved the streets with a thousand golden guineas." These guineas came from the pockets of the good citizens. In 1830 the town was transformed by the installation of gaslight in the streets and in some of the shops and houses. Ten years later there was an improvement in the roads, and a small coach 'The

Defiance' was running daily to Aberdeen, and also 'The Star' to Inverness. Travel was made easier and perhaps Janet was able to visit her family in Peebles. Her father died in 1833. William Chambers wrote:

> In his picturesque reminiscences of Tammas, my brother [Robert Chambers] has failed to notice a somewhat curious fact. The old worthy underwent a considerable softening in the last few years of his life; and the conversion was all the more remarkable in it being the result of reading a novel, '*Thaddeus of Warsaw*' which an aged lady had persuaded him to peruse. The noble and pathetic sentiments of Miss Porter in narrating the afflictions of her fictitious hero touched the heart of the old Puritan, and did what no power on earth had been able to effect.

John Russel was a faithful member of the Town Council for many years. He was elected bailie in 1807, and again in the years 1810, 1813 and 1816. In 1819 he was voted treasurer. However the next year there was a storm over the election of the Member of Parliament. The burgh, in common with four others, had the right to elect its own member.

The contest was between two leading families, the Duffs and the Grants. There were some dramatic irregularities. After a stormy campaign the Grant party unsuccessfully attempted to capture two councillors who were Duff supporters. This sparked off the capture of Mr Robert Dick, a Grant man. He was taken to Burghead and then over the Moray Firth and arrived back too late to cast his vote. On the same day a Duff supporter was seized and taken to Sutherland in a perilous journey when a storm blew up. He missed the vote. There were other alarms in the town over two days. When the results of the election were announced General Duff won by a vote, but after legal consultations this was disallowed and the Grant candidate was declared victorious. John Russel was on the Grant side. But through the self-electing process then in place, the council gradually eased out the Grant supporters and by 1822 was entirely pro-Duff. John Russel was replaced in 1821, and turned his back on the Town Council in disgust. He, together with his son Alexander, became an advocate of the reform of the system.

When the children John and Janet Russell moved from a house in the High Street to one in Academy Street, Margaret and Janet (Jessie) were educated at a private school run by a Miss Shand, and later took various posts as governesses. They paid frequent visits to relatives in Leith and Edinburgh, descendants from David Grieve of Jedderfield, but were always at home to help in times of need. In turn each of the boys left school and headed towards his chosen career. Thomas, the eldest, settled in Elgin and became a partner in the legal firm of Russell and Bain in Academy Street. In 1934 he married Charlotte Sutherland of Boharm; they rented a house in Moss Street and had one little girl, Jessie. Thomas seems to have been a generous man; there are records of loans he made to two young men, one who went to Sydney and the other to Montreal. The loans were not repaid.

In 1834 Thomas and his father entered into a business enterprise, which was to have considerable effect on the family. This was the purchase of the plant of the *Elgin Courier*. This weekly paper had been floated in July 1827 by John Grant, Bookseller, Stationer and Printer in Elgin. The circulation amounted to about 216 copies, and out of the 7d charged, 4d was taken in tax. In 1834 the press was shut down and for a few months Elgin was without a paper. The plant, which Thomas Russell bought was an "improved Columbian press of the largest dimensions". He wished to restart the paper under the name *The Elgin Courier*, but a Mr Peter Merson (who will become an important figure in our story) had bought the rights to that title and would not part with them. So the paper was launched in late 1834 under a new name.

New premises were needed for the business and John Russel bought Our Lady High House on the north side of the High Street about two hundred yards west of the Little Cross. The house was an ancient religious building and at one time a school had been held there by Sir Thomas Ragg. It was in a very decayed state and John had it pulled down. On the site he had extensive premises erected – on to the road he had a large two-storey printing house and offices and beyond it a pleasing dwelling house. On the west side of the courtyard he had two more houses and five small shops built. Which of the sons was to run this new enterprise?

Thomas was involved, but was already settled in his own legal business. The second son, James, had graduated at King's College, Aberdeen, and was licensed for the church. As there was no vacancy he took the post of schoolmaster at Knockando in Banffshire. John, the third son, set up as a merchant in Glasgow and it is said he married a Grieve cousin from Peebles, but he remains rather a shadowy figure. And the youngest of the family, Frank, went to train in offices in Edinburgh and subsequently in London, but later returned to Elgin. Janet's childhood had been a strict one, but her life in Elgin was a full one with many pleasures, interests and the satisfactions of being part of the successes of her husband and her children.

It is fortunate that I have been able to find out a great deal about my Russell family ancestors. However there is one stumbling block. Was John Russel related to the Russells of School Brae, Peebles? I will describe in an appendix my mother's and my granny's and my own attempts to piece together the jigsaw of this part of our family tree. The amateur genealogist faces strange pitfalls.

Gig for a Special Journey

CHART A: NOTES AND ABBREVIATED CHART OF THE RUSSELLS OF ALVES PARISH AND ELGIN, MORAY

There were Russell families in the farms of Easter and Wester Alves since the early 18th century with many OPR entries showing a Russell marrying a Russell. Also there is little variety in the Christian names. All this is confusing to the genealogist. A flat stone in the Alves churchyard is inscribed:

> JOHN RUSSEL late Tacksman of CARDON and COTES OF INNES who died May 1810 aged 87 and his wife ELSPETH GILLON who died 1785 aged 54 both natives of this parish and finally rested here as did their forefathers for several generations. JOHN RUSSEL a respectable farmer born in the reign of JAMES V1 being the ancestor of the family.

It is interesting to note that the name is spelled with one L and that my great-great-grandfather who was descended from this Cardon family continued to write his name Russel. The legend is that an Alexander Russell, a soldier who had fought at the battle of Marston Moor and was a Royalist, fled from the Border country, and came to Elgin in the 17th century. There are various testaments of Elgin families in the archives. However, Jane Russell, daughter of Francis Russell, one of the Elgin families, acquired the estate of Blackhall Aberdeenshire. Jane Russell's sister married Archibald Farquharson of Finzean. The interesting thing is that the motto of the Bedford Russell family, which was carved on the entry gates to Blackhall, (this carving is no longer there) shows a goat and the motto CHE SARA SARA. It is strange that this crest appears on the mural monument in the New Cemetery to my great-grandfather Alexander Russell, with no known explanation or authority. So there is one mystery.

The families who are descendants of the Blackhall Russells could not give me any further information (but that was in 1984). Nor have

I have been able to link the early Elgin Russells with the Russells of Alves. The other unsolved mystery is – why did John Russell go to Peebles? Were the two families connected? Now to facts!

CHART A: ABBREVIATED CHART OF MY RUSSELL ANCESTORS IN ALVES PARISH

James Russell 1743-1808 farmer in Cloves m. 24.12.1770 Margaret Russell b.1747 ch. two sons only, the second James 1774-? (unm.); the elder son:

  John Russel 1771-1847 merchant and Bailie in Elgin m.1806 Janet Russell of Peebles 1786-1874 (see Chart B, below) ch.

  1. Thomas Russell 1807-1840 merchant in Glasgow m.(no date) Charlotte Sutherland b.1811 ch.

      Jessie Russell 1835-1909 m.1824, m.1860 Franc Conquergood of Leith 1829-1911 ch:

      Isabella Conquergood 1865-1942 m.1895 Henry Charles Cameron 1856-1936 (descendants)

  2. James Russell 1809-1836 Rev. unm.

  3. Alexander Russell b. 1813 m. (see Chart D, Chapter 4)

  4. Margaret Russell 1815-1877 unm.

  5. Janet (Jessie) Russell 1818-1893 unm.

  6. Francis William (Frank) 1822-1861 Editor *Banffshire Journal* unm.

David Grieve in Jedderfield, Peebles, 1713-1787, son of John Grieve, Little Ormstoun, Peebles **m.25.11.1743 (1) Helen Gibson** ch.

(1) Hellen Grieve b. 1744 who by her second husband James Chambers was mother of William 1800-1883 and Robert Chambers 1802-1871, Edinburgh (2) Thomas 1746 (3) John 1748 (4) Jannet 1750

m.9.5.1754 (2) Margaret White 1733-1808 ch:

1.**Margaret Grieve 1755-1834 m. Thomas Russell (see below)**
2.Lillias Grieve b.1759
3.David Grieve b.1761 d.y.
4.William Grieve b.1764
5.David Grieve b.1766
6.Thomas Grieve 1769-1840 merchant, Edinburgh
7.Archibald Grieve b.1771 master builder, Stirling
8.James Grieve 1774 wright, Glasgow
9.Robert Grieve 1776-1853 of Noblehall, merchant, Edinburgh (see Chart E, Chapter 7)

Family of 1 above: Margaret Grieve 1755 m.21.6.1776 Thomas Russell 1751-1833, wheelwright in Peebles ch:
1.Margaret Russell b.1777 (d.y)
2.Rachel Russell b.1778 m. Bussells
3.Alexander (Sandy) Russell 1781-1861 wright in Peebles unm.
4.Elizabeth (Betty) Russell 1784-1863 unm.
5.**Janet Russell 1786-1874 m.1806 John Russel of Elgin** (see Chart A, above)
6.Barbara Russell 1789 m.1812 JohnVeitch
7.David Russell 1792-1825 unm.

8 . Margaret Russell b.1794
9. Lilias Russell b.1796
10.Joan Russell 1798-1860 m.1822 James Morrison, Peebles, five daughters and one son;
daughter Agnes Russell m. – Wallace (descendants USA)

CHAPTER 2

ALEXANDER RUSSELL AND THE MERSONS

It was Alexander, the third son, who became the proprietor and the editor of the new newspaper. He returned from training with an Edinburgh legal firm, settled in Elgin and was there for the rest of his life. From his obituary we learn of his career in journalism:

> It may be safely said that none worked harder – even in those days of hard newspaper work – than Mr Russell. He threw the whole of the energy of his nature into the management, and determined that he would make *The Courant* a power in the country. Many readers will know the success which crowned his efforts. It was during that time that *The Courant* had is greatest weight. There is no mistaking the views enunciated in its columns, the leading articles being terse, trenchant, and pointed, yet always gentlemanly and courteous. Himself a Conservative in politics, he found *The Courant* a Conservative paper, conducted it as a Conservative paper, and left it thus when he sold it in 1859. But Mr Russell was by no means a bigot, who could see no good in anyone holding differing opinions. He believed there were many good and honourable men who conscientiously differed from him.

Alex (as he was always known) kept the paper to a regular format; it consisted of half local and half national news. The editorials were usually on subjects of national importance, often on current political issues, and written in a plain unadorned style. An impressively large section on 'Foreign Intelligence' was matched by one headed 'Domestic Intelligence'. News of the Royal Family and events in London figured large. Obviously the people in this northerly burgh of 'North Britain' had an interest in what was going on in the faraway Metropolis. In May there were full reports of the proceedings at the General Assembly, and sometimes when Alex himself attended, the material was first-hand. There were notes on plays and players at the Edinburgh Theatre, and occasionally reports of current trials. Nearer to home regular features included Farming News and Markets, Lossiemouth Harbour, news from the Aberdeen Colleges, meetings of societies and, in great detail, reports of the monthly meetings of the Elgin Town Council. Obituaries were confined to announcements except when the deceased person was of some importance.

The extent of the book reviews amazed me; five to six books and periodicals were reviewed in each issue. Such books as Carson's *Bibliography of Sir Walter Scott* (1843), Longfellow's *Works*, the latest history books, and numerous religious books, most of them now forgotten. Each month the following journals were described: *Blackwoods Magazine, The Scottish Review, The Ladies Treasury, For Ladies of Middle Class Life*. Each week a poem was printed, usually giving the author's name, but one is anonymous. I can't help wondering if Alex wrote it.

The Dreamer

Not in the laughing bowers,
Where, by the great twining boughs, a pleasant shade
A summer noon is made
But where the incessant din
Of iron hands, and roar of brazen throats
Join their unmingling notes,
While the long summer day is pouring
Til day is done and darkness does begin
Dream I – and yet I dream
Dream what – If man were more just
I might have been.
How strong and fair, how kindly and serene

Glowing of heart and glorious of mien,
The conscious crown of Nature's blissful scene
In just and equal brotherhood I glean,
With all mankind, exhaustless pleasures keen
Such is my dream.

It was said that Alex Russell was sensitive to the needs of others, and was always concerned about the poor. He became a member of the Town Council and through his newspaper and council work he got to know almost every family in and around Elgin.

From his reading he learned a good deal about conditions of those who worked in factories, and of the state of housing in city slums. He was soon joined in the business by his young brother Frank, who was interested in literature, and probably wrote the book reviews. Some reports were in a florid Victorian style such as the following:

The Academy Ball, September 30th 1840

> The students of the Academy gave their annual ball on Friday last, 23rd inst, and seldom have we witnessed a more delightful scene than the Trinity Lodge Association Rooms exhibited on that occasion. The company present, of all ages, exceeded 300, and the display of youthful beauty was such that the strangers present all acknowledged that they had scarcely seen anything like it. Nothing could surpass the spirit in which the dancing was held, while the juvenile part of the assembly entered into the entertainment with all the full abandonment of youth which only the young can feel. The smile on the aged face expressed a more chastened, but no less heart-felt, sympathy in their enjoyment. Enhanced by the presence of a party from Gordon Castle – their Graces the Duke and Duchess of Richmond, Lady Caroline Gordon-Lennox, the Earl of March, Lord Fitzroy Gordon-Lennox and other youthful guests. The frankness and urbanity of his Grace, and the kind interest the Duchess took in the young people around her made a deep impression on the hearts of young and old alike.

In October 1836 John Russel had his sixty-fifth birthday. In the thirty years since he and his bride Janet had driven up from Peebles in a gig, they had celebrated two hundred and sixteen family birthdays. The fate of their place by birth and their own exertions had given them a good and prosperous life, and now all augured well. They must have hoped for good marriages for their children and joy from grandchildren yet to come. Instead disaster struck.

Their second son James fell ill and came from Knockando to be nursed at home. He died on 3 December 1836. We have an obituary from the paper:

> Died here on 3rd Inst in the twenty-eighth year of his age, the Rev. James Russell, schoolmaster in Knockando, a young man of the most amiable disposition, unaffected piety, and engaging manners. Acceptable as a preacher of the Gospel and efficient as an instructor of youth; dutiful as a son, and attached in the highest degree as a friend, his memory will live long in the affectionate remembrance, not only as the writer of this brief tribute to his memory, but to all who had the pleasure of his acquaintance.

We will never know what was the cause of his death. But that was only the beginning of a continuing tragedy. In the west end of the cathedral ruins there is a recumbent slab inscribed as follows:

IN MEMORY OF THE REV. JAMES RUSSELL

SCHOOLMASTER IN KNOCKANDO WHO DEPARTED

THIS LIFE 3RD DECEMBER 1836 IN THE

28TH YEAR OF HIS AGE

AND OF HIS BROTHER THOMAS RUSSELL

WRITER IN ELGIN WHO DIED THE 23RD

DECEMBER 1840 AGED 33 YEARS

AND THEIR BROTHER JOHN RUSSELL

MERCHANT IN GLASGOW WHO DIED AT

ELGIN ON THE 3RD OCTOBER 1845

AGED 34.

You will notice that each of the sons died in Elgin. Thomas had married Charlotte Sutherland, and Jessie, their only child, was just over a year old when he died. If these three brothers died of tuberculosis, there is no trace of it in the succeeding generations.

John and Janet must have been comforted by the love of their two daughters and of Alexander and Frank. John himself died on 24 May 1847. He was 77 years old. There is a recumbent slab in his name next to that of his sons. A true son of his father, Alex took over the post of treasurer to the Guildry; he held it for thirty-one years. He settled debts owing to the firm of Russell and Bain, unpaid loans, which the generous Thomas had made to two young men in order that they might emigrate, and he made sure Charlotte was not burdened. He comforted his mother and sisters and took his place as head of the sadly depleted family.

I would now like to introduce another Elgin family, the Mersons. Peter Merson has already been mentioned as Master of the Mathematical School at Elgin Academy. He was born in Huntley, the son of John Merson who was blacksmith to the Duke of Huntley. Peter and his brother William turned out to be the academics of the family and had a life-long friendship, each of them qualifying for the church at Aberdeen University. Peter gained a reputation as a scholar early; such was his prowess at the local school that at the age of thirteen he sat the examinations for King's College Aberdeen and came out overall first with top honours in Latin. After three years at King's he spent six months as assistant teacher at Fochabers School. Then a vacancy for sole charge at the school at Rothiemay came up. There were several applications, but such was the reputation of Peter Merson that they all withdrew. The Presbytery paid him a high compliment.

My brother and I visited Rothiemay recently. This lovely peaceful village is several miles up the River Deveron from Huntly. We saw the site of the old school. We visited the churchyard, and read the inscription on a handsome stone to the Simmie family. From *The Courant's* obituary to Peter we have: "Dr Simmie took a great fancy to the young schoolmaster and acted as a father to him, a kindness Mr

Merson never forgot, but delighted to his dying day to speak of the talented and kind-hearted minister of Rothiemay."

In his time there Peter taught the four older Simmie children, Margaret, Anne, Keturah and David. When I read the name KETURAH on the gravestone I felt a moving sense of the wonder and the sadness in family history, in reflecting on what is destiny, what is chance, what is freedom of choice. I stood there by the grave, my mind and feelings in the past, with the heavy knowledge of what was to come.

While Peter was in Rothiemay he studied for the degree in divinity, which he later obtained. He then took the post of tutor to the sons of Colonel Grant at Redcastle in the south of the Black Isle. He had been licensed by the Presbytery of Strathbogle, and was preaching at Killearnan on the day that the Battle of Waterloo was fought. He later remarked that so slow was the communication in this remote part of Scotland the news of the victory was not received there for another eight weeks!

It seems that Peter had doubts as to whether he should go into the ministry or into teaching. He returned to Aberdeen in 1816 and there set up 'Mr Merson's Private Academy' in the Netherkirkgate, and he had "no little success in preparing boys for the University". At the same time he undertook the Herculean task of rearranging the books (which had all gone to confusion) at the Theological Hall at Marischal College. Meantime his brother William had obtained his degree and was employed as assistant to Mr Mowat at the Grammar School in St Andrews. While there he attended classes at St Mary's College, took his degree and was licensed in 1815. He became tutor to the sons of Colonel Glass at Abbey Park. He then obtained the living at Crail Church, and later married Jessie, daughter of Colonel Glass. So there was a link between Elgin, St Andrews and Crail, a link that has continued up to this day.

During the time when Peter was running his school in Aberdeen he met Miss Eliza Smith. She was the only child of Charles Smith, part

Eliza Merson (née Smith), from a portrait   *Peter Merson of Elgin Academy*

owner of the Stoneywood Paper Works at Dyce, and his wife Barbara Gordon from the Cabrach. If you have never been to the Cabrach you should go. It is a remote upland village of farms, and seems to have changed less than have most places.

I have a series of letters, left by my grandmother; they are from Alex Smith of Kinellar, a next generation cousin of the Stoneywood Smiths. I quote from one letter:

> I used to hear my father tell of the courting days of Eliza Smith, and she had many suitors. I wonder if you ever heard of the time that she was given up for lost? There was no railway or steamship in those days, and she had been invited by some friends to make at trip to London. The London smack was driven off its course by a storm, and there were six weeks that they were never heard of.

Of the many suitors for Eliza's hand, Peter Merson was the successful man. In 1821 he applied for and secured the post of the

Mathematical School at Elgin Academy. On 5th of November of that year he and Eliza Smith were married at Stoneywood House. (But this is not the very fine Stoneywood House which was built by the Piries in 1850, and which is now used by ARJO WIGGINS, the owners of the mills, as a guest house for visitors. The old Stoneywood House – or what remains of it – is now part of the mills, and was built in 1683.) Charles Moir inherited it, and also from a Charles Smith letter we read "My father used to show me the secret room where Charles Moir, who was a Jacobite, hid until he made his escape to Norway. There he stayed until he was pardoned for his part in the 1745 Jacobite rebellion." In 1800 Charles Smith and a cousin Alexander Smith inherited the mills, Charles taking the upper mills and living in the old Stoneywood House. Again from an Alex Smith (Kinellar) letter we have a moving description of a scene, which took place in that house. Both the old house and the one that the Piries built stand high over the River Don.

'I remember quite distinctly Mrs Smith's death in the old mansion of Stoneywood. My mother and Mrs Smith were very friendly, and I, as a child between three and four years of age, was often there. There was a window looked out onto the Don, and I can remember sitting there looking at the water as it rushed along. I think my mother dressed Mrs Smith in her death robe. I remember being there all day with my mother, and being lifted up to see my old friend sleeping, and was asked to put my hand upon her head and feel how cold it was. It was the first time I had looked on death. My mother, who had a great regard for Mrs Smith, said she believed she died of a broken heart.'

The troubles began when young Mr Pirie inherited the lower mills and set on a course of action to take over all of them. There was a succession of lawsuits, which finally broke Charles Smith. The capitulation must have been grievous to all of the Smith family. After Mrs Smith's burial at Dyce, Charles Smith agreed to go and live with Peter and Liza Merson in Elgin. Family stories, by their very nature, branch out and go back and forward in time. So let us go back to Elgin and take up the story from the time Eliza Smith settled with her husband Peter Merson in Elgin.

Keturah Merson, needlework portrait by her sister Mina, c.1840

CHART C: ABBREVIATED CHART OF MERSON FAMILY

John Merson b.1747 blacksmith in Huntley m. 19.12.1786 Janet Mitchell b.1754 ch:
1. James Merson 1787-1811
2. Peter Merson (Rev.) 1789-1820 (see below)
3. John Merson 1790-1865
4. William Merson (Rev. Minister Crail) 1792-1865 m. Jessie Grant Glass, St Andrews
5. Janet Merson 1795-1892 m. James Robson blacksmith

Family of 2 above:
Rev. Peter Merson (Elgin Academy) 1780-1867 m. 1821 Elizabeth Smith b.1791 (daughter of Charles Smith 1767-1846, paper manufacturer of Stoneywood, Aberdeenshire, and Barbara Gordon 1763-1844 of Oldtown, Cabrach) ch:
1. Charles (Rev.) Merson 1822-1869
2. Jannet (Jessie) Merson 1824-1917 unm.
3. Elizabeth Langlands Merson 1826-1853 unm.
4. Barbara Gordon Merson 1828-1896 unm.
5. Williamina Grant Glass Merson 1830-1915 m. 21.8.1859 Captain Sim
6. **Keturah Gerard Simmie Merson 1832-1854 m.1951 Alexander Russell (see Chart D, Chapter 4)**

CHAPTER 3

THE MERSONS AND A MARRIAGE

My feeling is that the new young Mrs Peter Merson was a loving, tolerant wife, a good mother and a pleasing organiser of the social life of the family. Peter was soon respected and admired in Elgin. Quoting briefly from the long obituary in *The Courant*:

> A whole generation grew up about him in Elgin. Four years after he had taken up the post of Master of the Mathematical School, the post of Master of the Classical School fell empty, and he was invited to move over. However he decided to stay where he was, "preferring" he said "the exact sciences". His kind heart and his kind language gained for him the strong love of his pupils, who questioned him when opportunity served as if he had been their father, and he was ever ready to help a boy out of difficulties. While conducting his department he never sent out a scholar who would say an unkind or a derogatory word about him. When he came to Elgin he established a new institution in connection with the Academy. Like other men of his native glens he was very fond of dancing, and at once set about getting up an Academy Ball. A grand ball came off in the year 1821, Mr Merson presiding. This he did for about forty years, as a whim always in the same slippers, which are still preserved as curiosities. He might be seen, year after year, standing in the centre of a group of ladies and gentlemen, who all entertained a profound respect for him. The smile was ever on his face. His racy humour spread pleasure all about him.

Eliza and Peter were blessed with good fortune in their family life. They had a family of six; Charles was the first born, and the youngest, a girl, was born on 23 June 1832. There was a fine gathering at the baptism. Peter's brother William travelled all the way from Crail to perform the ceremony. The name the baby girl was given was Keturah

Gerard Simmie Merson. The witnesses were Mr and Mrs Walker, Bailies Cormie and Anderson, the Reverend James Jenkins, Mr William Smith, Mrs Cormie and Mrs Anderson. In retrospect the event was important to me: this was my great-grandmother, and she was the first Keturah in our family. The name has been given to girls in our families for five generations – in Britain, Australia and now in Canada. (In case you are wondering who was the first-known Keturah, it was the name of Abraham's second wife.)

Keturah Russell (née Merson), shadow portrait, 1854

Peter must have found it hard on a schoolmaster's salary to keep the household at 10 North Street in the style to which his wife was accustomed. He was an energetic and hard-working man, and apart from being clerk to the Presbytery, he also held the post of the chaplaincy to the prison, that of Inspector of Weights and Measures, the clerkship to the Teinds Court, and he was an actuary to the Elgin Savings Bank and an insurance agent. It was written, 'He carried out all these duties with the zest and competence which characterised him'.

Peter continued to help his father-in-law with the troubles at Stoneywood, but was personally also affected, as he had taken the lease of barnyards and maltings on the estate. The entire correspondence with Sir James Hay is in a printed booklet. I will quote a small item, which indicates Peter Merson's character. "I wish for nothing except what is strictly consistent with justice … I ask for the appointment of a judicious arbiter, being anxious to avoid a law suit because I conceive that the facts and pleadings adduced in court seldom reflect much credit upon any of the parties, but afford abundant food for petty scandal and high amendment to clerks, newspaper reporters and others."

During all the anxious waiting time (and others later), Eliza kept the household running serenely and smoothly. From her portrait she has a look of strength and endurance. From 1834 to 1848 Peter Merson was engaged in a dispute with the town council. Matters of principle were at stake, and in his capacity as clerk to the Presbytery he fought a two-fold battle. The background was as follows: Elgin Academy was built in 1801 to replace the old Grammar School and the English School. The total cost was covered by subscriptions from the public. An agreement was made whereby the Presbytery continued to hold its previous superintendence of the schools by retaining the right to interview and approve the teaching posts. Those appointed had to be members of the Church of Scotland. It was also the Presbytery, which named the dates of examination, examined the three schools of the Academy, presented the prizes and fixed the dates of the holidays. The council administered the upkeep of the buildings, appointed the teachers and paid their salaries.

At the time of the Disruption in May 1843, the current minister, Mr Topp, and about twelve hundred others left St Giles and formed their own congregation. Soon the injustice of the rule that only members of the Established Church might be appointed as teachers to the Academy and other schools was strongly felt, and the council appointed two masters who were dissenters. Most of the members of the town council had joined the new church. At first cautiously and then recklessly the councillors set about taking full control of the Academy. It was apparent that Peter Merson was to be the main obstacle in their path. He had certain qualities, which made him admirably suited to play the major role in a case that eventually went to the House of Lords. He respected truth and justice; his mind was quick and clear on any legal matter, and once fired by a case, he had a spirit of dogged determination. He seems to have retained optimism that the power of reason and logic would sway his opponents.

The entire papers of the long dispute are available in the archives at Elgin. One of the dramas fully reported in *The Courant* was that in 1846 the council flung down the gauntlet: without consulting the Presbytery nor advising the masters, it set the dates for their own examination, announced the Provost would present the prizes, and gave out dates for holidays different from those already set by the Presbytery. When the Presbytery party arrived to conduct the usual examination, they found the doors of the English and Latin schools locked. At this point Peter Merson drew up a document of objection, which he then presented to the council, refusing to let them examine his classes. It began: "I Peter Merson – do hereby object to the intimation recently published in *The Courant* – for the following reasons." Here followed eleven reasons based on the legal aspects of the matter as established by long practice. The council then published a long statement condemning the behaviour of Mr Merson.

Notices in *The Courant* at the beginning of June 1847 made it plain that the council was taking the same course as in the previous year. Peter Merson wrote to the council making it plain that he would not comply. An extract from the letter states "I have only further to mention that I adhere to the whole terms of my protest, and that any examination to which I may subject my pupils on Tuesday or Wednesday must be held and received as a matter of courtesy and not obligation."

There being no reply, on the Wednesday Peter sent a further note while examinations were proceeding in the Latin School. The Town Clerk was sent with a verbal message that the Provost would proceed, and if Mr Merson were not there with his pupils it would be "to his own Peril".

"This is a matter of conscience," Mr Merson replied.

"No," said Mr Duff, "the Patrons claim it as a matter of right and require you to act accordingly."

Mr Merson turned to his class. "Boys, you may dismiss," he said.

Mr Duff countered this. "Boys," he said, "don't make fools of yourselves and your master, but remain here."

Mr Merson continued instructing his pupils and then the Provost and party walked in. "It is very unhandsome of you to presume to do this," said Mr Merson, and walked out.

Of course his job was on the line. The council sought legal advice, but were loath to dismiss such a respected master. Instead they withheld his salary. For a time he was forced to submit and apologise, but he continued to investigate legal aspects and wrote a fresh protest the next summer. On 19 June Peter received a letter asking him to meet the Magistrates that evening to arrange the examination. He replied to the effect that he meant to adhere to the whole terms of his protest. When the examiners entered his schoolroom the Provost asked for the examination to begin. "I take no orders from you Sir," said Mr Merson, "I take orders from the Presbytery," and he left the room. The council had no alternative; at the meeting next day the vote was cast in favour of the motion that Mr Merson be dismissed. He was informed and replied that he intended to contest his dismissal in the courts. The council decided it would defend its rights. On 31 July Peter Merson brought a suspension and interdict from the Court of Session. Pending the interdict he was to continue in his post. On 19 February the next year the case of Mr Merson was remitted by the Lord Ordinary to the Inner House. However, it was soon intimated that the Presbytery of Elgin was going to take legal action against the council. Part of the grounds was that the council had illegally appointed to the Latin and English Schools masters who had not subscribed to the Confession of Faith. A test case was to be fought asserting the Presbytery's rights of superintendence.

The years rolled by with tedious delays. News of the final decision in the Academy case reached Elgin in January 1861. The Lords of the First Division of the Court of Session unanimously declared against the council. Elgin Academy under the terms of its foundation fell within the jurisdiction, superintendence and control of the Presbytery. It was exactly as Peter Merson had argued from the start. But the council decided to appeal to the House of Lords. The final decision came swiftly. The House of Lords upheld the decision of the Lords of the Court of Session. Elgin Council was in serious financial difficulties. But the case served to highlight the need for reform of the law, and in August 1872 an Act of Parliament was passed that entirely severed all burgh schools from the Church.

At this point I must interrupt to pay respects to John Russel, who died on 24 May 1847, and was buried in the cathedral ruins near the grave of his sons. One would have expected a long obituary in *The Courant*, but there is only a short notice. Did Alex feel that, in his position as proprietor and editor of the paper, it was not good taste to extol his father? I am sure there was a big assembly at his funeral, and I know that Alex was a great comfort to his widowed mother.

To return to 9 North Street and Peter and Eliza's family, in June 1849 the youngest of the family, Keturah, or Tudy as they called her, had completed her schooling. She was very beautiful with fair hair and brown eyes, regular features and a shy smile. Jessie was now twenty-five, kind hearted but short-tempered, and from the age of sixteen had been governess to the children of the Johnstones of Lesmurdie. Barbara, blonde, good-natured, reserved, had a similar post with an English family. The three youngest girls of the family were at home. Eliza was full of fun and eager for life, Mina, skilled in needlework, and enterprising. Their mother involved them in the social life of the town, and in charitable work, and encouraged the expression of their individual talents, in Tudy's case in drawing and singing.

Alexander Russell, as a friend of Peter and Eliza, was a frequent visitor at the Merson's house at 10 North Street. At the end of November the following letter arrived for Mrs Merson's attention:

Courant Office
Elgin. 38 November 1849

My Dear Mrs Merson,

I have for some time been waiting for an opportunity of speaking to you privately regarding a matter in which you are deeply interested; but I have not yet been so fortunate as to find you alone. I cannot, however, delay in informing you of what has taken place between your daughter Keturah and myself. I have for a considerable time conceived a warm attachment to her, which on our more intimate acquaintance rapidly gained strength till I felt called upon to make advances to her, which she received with the utmost esteem and affection; and after several private interviews, we pledged ourselves to each other, in the hope and confidence that you and Mr. M. will give your most hearty concurrences. We are in no particular hurry, and I have merely written this note because I think it is my duty to inform you of the matter as early as possible, and also in order that you may give me an opportunity of an interview with you, when I could state my mind more fully and satisfactorily than in writing. I sincerely hope that this communication will be received by you in the same spirit in which it is written and that you will cordially co-operate with us about a happy consummation of our most earnest wishes.

I will likely be with you tonight after the meeting of the club, when if you think it proper you can let me know your mind on the subject.

I am,
My Dear Mrs Merson,
Yours most sincerely,
Alexr. Russell

There was not a moment to show the letter to Peter, for he came in late, ate with the family, and left immediately. Before his return Eliza hustled the girls off to their rooms, and was pleased to see Alex arrive with Peter. She left the drawing room on some pretext, and awaited the outcome.

There is an aspect of Peter's character that has not yet been described. Quoting again from his obituary: "We have to say that one of the strongest features of Mr Merson's character was a childlike simplicity of heart, a thing found in conjunction with the most profound learning and intellectual power." This simplicity was illustrated in Peter's reaction to Alexander's request, as related by my grandmother many years later. Mrs Merson, returned to the room, having judged there had been plenty of time for discussion, and heard her husband say, in tones of profound astonishment and dismay, "Oh no, no NO, not my wee Tudy – she's no' but a bairn," and then, after a short pause, "Would ye no' tak Jessie?"

No doubt Mrs Merson brought common sense and reality, permission was given, and Alex proposed to Tudy. He was accepted, but it was agreed not to make the engagement public for a

Alexander Russell, Elgin, from a portrait

while. Tudy was just seventeen, Alex was thirty-two. And after all, he had said there was "no particular hurry".

The reader will now understand the important part the Merson family played in my story. For the time being the engagement was not announced. Two letters written in 1860 were carefully kept, and handed down by my grandmother to her daughter and then to myself. These were sent by Alex to Tudy, who was dispatched to stay first with her brother Charles Merson, minister at Arbroath, and then with her Uncle William Merson, minister at Crail in Fife. The Mersons at Crail had a son Andrew, who was at that time studying at St Andrews University. His course comprised the following subjects: Latin, Mathematics, Logic, Ethics, and Philosophy of the Senses. No doubt he enjoyed meeting his young cousin from Elgin. So here is the letter, now 153 years old.

Courant Office
Elgin, 17th May/50

My Dearest Tudy,

You see I don't delay long in answering your welcome note of Wednesday. I suppose that when you wrote it I was at a Protection Meeting at Banff. I was sent to attend there on Wednesday and of course could not refuse the call. I went by coach on Wednesday morning and returned by the same conveyance that evening, but being only three hours there and busy all the time, I did not get out to see about me.

There are lots of evening parties here at present. On Friday we were at the Sellars, but no ladies invited, there was little fun and too much punch. On Sunday I was at the Carlie's new lodgings. On Monday evening we had a concert at the conclusion of which I gave a soiree to the McWilliams, McPherson, McBey, Dr Robertson, Mr Dempster and the 'Carlie'. On Wednesday we were asked to three parties, first to meet the Mrs Clark and Mrs Murdoch at no. 9 North Street, but that would not do and your Mama excused us. How could we meet Miss Murdoch after what she had been so wicked in circulating? We were then asked to the Audsleys where my sister and Frank went, and enjoyed themselves till past two next morning. I could not think of going although I was home in time, as I had a good deal of writing in hand and too little time to accomplish it.

Now for something soft. The chief reason of my asking you to let me know your plans was my position in reference to my little nephew. I promised to meet my aunt halfway to take him to Elgin and it is now past the time proposed. I had a letter from her on Monday morning wondering that I had not written to her on the subject. I had therefore no alternative but to tell her plainly that cause of our delay, which was that I expected our marriage to take place early in July, and as were to go south at that time, we could then take my nephew home with us – I thought that I would thus make one errand of both matters. As however that cannot be (my aunt having to go to the country for her health). I have been cogitating the best plan of getting the laddie here, and must write her the result in a day or two. So you see how I have been situated.

I observe what you say about your delicacy in writing upon the subject and also you stiffness. I had thought that from our intercourse and my own open-mindedness to you that both these had left you for ever. I am sure you have nothing to fear from me and you should at once open your mind and heart fully and freely, and I trust you will find me worthy of your confidence, love and esteem. That is my feeling towards you, and I have no doubt you reciprocate it. As to your dread of my friends, I shall only say that you will be most agreeably disappointed, for I am certain they will receive you with open arms and warm hearts. Were it otherwise, you might surely depend on me for every support against all and sundry. Do, my Dearest Tudy, banish from your mind all groundless fears, and I have no doubt, should it please Providence that we should be united, we will be both happy and comfortable. You know well my deep affection for you and I have the vanity to believe that you love me warmly. I miss your society terribly just now and the last few weeks have seemed like months, but never mind that. Enjoy yourself while you can as a lass, for you will soon have to Assume the functions of a Wife.

I leave you now to fix a time and would wish to know it as soon as possible, as I have several arrangements to make which will require time.

I am, Dearest Keturah,
Yours affectionately
Alexr. Russell

So Tudy was away for some weeks. So it seems there had been gossip. So it seems that Tudy was still unsure – perhaps not of Alex, but of herself. Her father had said she was still a baby. Were these friends of Alex also friends of her parents? As to the reference to the little boy: John Smith was the son of a cousin of Janet Russell from Peebles (the mother of Alex). This cousin was Helen Grieve who married Edward Young of Melrose Castle and Jamaica. Edward died in Jamaica, and Helen and the little boy came back to Edinburgh. Helen took the post of matron at a school there, and it seems that her mother may have looked after the boy, but was not well. Alex gladly took him into his household, soon regarded him as a son, and was a strong influence in the distinguished career John Young was to follow.

What a welcome there was for Tudy on her return to Elgin. And what preparations for the great day! There were almost too many helpful hands in making the trousseau. I have a white handkerchief made for the bride; it has a wide border of handmade lace. The name Keturah is embroidered on one corner. There is also a small square piece from the wedding dress; the custom was that this was cut from the dress and attached to the bonnet to be worn to church on the first Sunday after the wedding.

The ceremony took place at 9 North Street on 12 August 1850. William Merson and Tudy's brother Andrew conducted the service. The drawing room was packed with parents, sisters, brothers and friends. Everyone was delighted with the match. Alex and Tudy spent their honeymoon in Edinburgh and Peebles. They first stayed at the Waverley Hotel in Princes Street. From the windows they could look down on the new railway and on Waverley Station. The *Scotsman* of 20 May 1948 gives a description of the first train from Glasgow. "A train with twenty locomotives emerged from the tunnel at the West Church (St Cuthberts) and proceeded slowly along the valley of the Nor' Loch, through the tunnel under the Mound, to the station of the North British Railway in the old Physics Gardens."

This was the time of railway fervour; the first train on the east coast route ran on 8 August. But the railway had not yet reached Peebles, and Alex and Tudy travelled thence on Mr Croall's coach, advertised as "having the capacity to cover the journey in three hours, horses changed thrice on the road". Alex was delighted to present his bride to all his Peebles relatives.

On their return to Elgin, Tudy assumed the 'duties of a wife' at their dear little four-square stone-built house. It is still occupied, but some of what was a green space to the north as far as the river Lossie has been built on. There were two maids in the household, both of them older than their mistress. And of course John Young, who was newly seven. I hope Tudy settled down happily and enjoyed her new family life and the cheerful social life of Elgin.

CHAPTER 4

ALEXANDER AND KETURAH RUSSELL

The decade 1850-1860 was referred to later by Browning as "glad confident morning". The machine age was in full swing, methods of production were being revolutionised, wages had increased, and there was more chance than ever before of a man being able to better himself. Of great importance was the unity brought about by a common belief, held by people of all classes, in a moral law, which was based on duty and self-restraint. Dr Samuel Smiles of London propounded a new philosophy, based on *Self Help*. Quoting from him: "All life is a struggle, competitive struggle is of prime importance. Workmen must work hard for increased wages, and masters work hard for the highest profits. There is provision for all, but to obtain work is essential." The virtues of saving were extolled. "And the sum of all this effort? The Nation depends on it: on individual industry, energy and uprightness."

Peace reigned and the future looked golden. There was a general pride in Britain and the glorious Empire. Asa Briggs wrote, "England was the world's workshop, the world's shipbuilders, the world's carriers and the world's clearing house. Business and farming were thriving, everyone was benefiting from the railway system." Briggs considered class system as a great asset to the unity of the nation. The children sang:

> *The rich man in his castle*
> *The poor man at his gate*
> *God made them high and lowly*
> *And ordered their estate.*

But there were those who recognised that there was some fearful poverty, and shocking conditions in housing both in cities and towns. 1851 was the year of the Great Exhibition at what was to be known as the Crystal Palace. Amazing that Joseph Paxton's Great Exhibition Hall, built of prefabricated glass and units of iron and steel (there were thirty-three thousand columns and two thousand three hundred girders) was assembled in seventeen weeks. In the centre of the Great Hall was a huge glass fountain. A transparent curtain of water flowed down over the invisible structure, which held three fluted basins of decreasing size. This waterfall fascinated the crowds of spectators who gathered around it. An important exhibit designed by Prince Albert was that of model dwelling houses for workers. It created much interest, but did not bring about much practical result. Flourishing charities provided for some of society's unfortunate people. Enlightened ideas and official spending were improving the provision for paupers and for lunatics. "Adversity," wrote Carlyle, "is sometimes hard upon a man; but for one man who can stand prosperity, there are a hundred who will stand adversity."

With this glimpse of the philosophy of the time, I would like to quote a sentence from Alexander Russell's obituary. "While to the indolent and thriftless he would administer well-earned rebuke, he was always ready to help adopt every method that would tend to the comfort of those unfortunate persons whom necessity threw upon the poor rates, and equally to adopt all the means that would discourage the profligate." This may seem pompous, but in the light of what Alexander achieved, and from what I learned of him from my grandmother, he was certainly not that.

Alexander also enjoyed his leisure, for example at the Masonic Ball. Think of him dancing with his lovely young wife, the Polka, the Mazurka, the Lancers and the Masons' Reel, which Alexander described as "striking metal into the heels of the dancers". But the time soon came when Tudy did not go to the dances and the parties. No doubt Miss Murdoch passed round the whispered word that young

Mrs Russell was in an interesting condition. Of course when they heard the news, Tudy's parents and her sisters, and Alex's mother and his brother Frank were all delighted. The ladies helped willingly to prepare the layette. The list was as follows: 12 robes, 12 white petticoats, 12 flannels, 2 cloaks, binders, 12 night caps, 12 shirts, 12 head flannels, 3 shawls, and a stack of hand stitched napkins. All this was assembled, and prudently laid ready by early August.

The tenth of August was a great day in Elgin, the day of the opening of the Morayshire railway. That evening Alexander sat up late writing his account of it.

> At length the steam is up and we are off for a ride on the Rail. Hundreds are gazing on us as we shoot along, impelled in the hot haste of the roaring, rushing monster as it steams and smokes, snorts and shrieks, rattles and rushes on its way. Some are promising that if we reach our journey's end in safety, they will themselves venture the perils of the "Rail", and resign themselves to the tender mercy of imprisoned steam. Others are inwardly vowing, more energetically than holily, that they will never, while sane. Full of reveration for their own young times, they regard the whole affair as a sin against Providence, as embodied forth in lean horses and plethoric coaches, and would not wonder if a special earthquake were to swallow up the train, and the seas were to come with double force to Spynie, and wash away the rails. Here we reach the mail road raised seven feet high for the railway's convenience. The first mail coach was started in 1812, and the blast of its horn as it entered the town of Elgin with a couple of horses and a guard with royal livery, excited no small interest and was held as the harbinger of a new era. How much more would you hail this train of flying carriages drawn by one huge iron horse, as the dawn of an era you could not dream of?

Just over a month later, on 19 September 1851, Tudy was safely delivered of a baby daughter. Alex was summoned to the bedroom, and the baby was placed gently in his arms. He was amazed at how small and how perfect she was. He held her close, then gave her to his dearest wife to hold. He took his gold watch from his pocket and put it by the baby's face. "See Tudy," he said, "her face is no bigger than the face of my watch," and he bent down and kissed the little girl, and then his young wife.

Uncle William came up from Crail to baptise the baby Keturah Elizabeth Russell. Frank, Charles Merson and the two grandmamas stood as witnesses. Tudy felt well, and made plans to embroider needlepoint covers for the set of six dining room chairs. The baby delighted them all. Her presence seemed to fill the house, dominating the thoughts and affections of everyone who was there. Her aunties came, bearing gifts. John Young came home from school with a handsome rattle he had bought with his pocket money. He and little Keturah made bonds that lasted throughout their long lives. Alex was in high spirits, coming through from his office on any pretext to admire his daughter.

In the April of the next year, 1852, Tudy was expecting another baby. A son was born on 13 December 1852, and was baptised John Patrick Merson Russell by his Uncle Charles. There was great rejoicing – here was a boy to carry on the Russell name. Little Keturah was fifteen months old. There were many eager offers of help.

And now the story, which has been such a happy one, changes. Tudy's closest sister, Liza, was ill, and died in March 1853. A year later Tudy gave birth to a second son, Charles William. She was slow to recover, was tired and listless. Her mother came to see her twice each day, and grew increasingly anxious. One morning, three weeks after the confinement, she spoke to Tudy, saying, "What – Tudy dear, are you still in bed? You should get up for a wee bit this afternoon. You will feel better for making the effort." And so, later in the day, Tudy was dressed and in the sitting room. There she was seized with a stroke and died immediately.

In the midst of his anguish, Alex realised that there was no picture of his wife. He summoned a man who made a shadow portrait of her. She lay in peace upon the bed, her golden hair smooth to her head, her eyes closed in the long, long sleep. As was the custom, Alex took his little daughter to say goodbye to her mother. Keturah struggled from his arms, ran to the bed and tried to seize her mother's hand. "Speak Mama, speak," she cried, and was afraid. Alex took her in his arms and vowed to himself that he would forever do his best to make up to her for this dreadful loss.

It seems likely that Margaret, Alex's sister, moved into Courant Court to run the house. The new baby was taken to be nursed at Allarburn Farm, a mile or so west of Elgin. Although he was breast-fed and tended well, he died when he was four months old. His name, together with that of his young mother's, is inscribed on a slab in Elgin Cathedral ruins. It is close to the slab of John Russel and his sons. Little Keturah was confused by the various images of death she acquired in her childhood, and the fear of death stayed with her all her life. She formed an idea of two fathers, one her own loving papa, and the other her Heavenly Father who had caused them all such grief by taking away to his house in the clouds Aunt Eliza, her mama and Grandmama Russell's 'three bonny laddies'. She was told that some day she would again be with mama, and, as all her mother's clothes were stored away in a big trunk, she had the hopeful idea that some day mama would come back home.

Meantime there was love and comfort from papa, Grandmama Russell, dear Uncle Frank, granny and grandpapa Merson and the kind aunties. She and Johnnie used to play games with Jane and Jessie, the maids; the favourite one was Honeypots. There was now a swing in the garden, and Keturah loved to be pushed higher and higher – perhaps mama in heaven would see her.

Time drove on. For Alexander it was marked by the inexorable rhythm of *The Courant's* week, with the gradual run-up to the hectic pre-publishing day on Thursday. There was a roundabout of meetings to attend – those of the Gas Light Company, the Lossiemouth Harbour Board, the Parochial Council, the Guildry Fund, the Water Company, the meeting of the Kirk Session. Now his work and his family life were separate, except for John Young's increasing interest in what was happening in the far-flung Empire. Alex seemed to be forever in a hurry, to be working late at night. But this helped to ease his grief. Passing time was space in which to recover.

The Crimean war ran its bitter course. War reports from William Russell a journalist, who had no connection with our family, brought to the public the fearful recognition of the disasters, of the chaos of organisation, the privations, the sufferings, the needless deaths. Indignation and anger mounted, and Lord John Russell the Prime Minister was forced to resign. There was a series of governmental changes and eventually Lord Palmerston seemed to take a more hopeful control. In the evenings Alex read some of the news to John Young, and there grew in the boy an increasing interest and admiration for Miss Florence Nightingale, which was to shape his distinguished career. In September 1855 it seemed that the war was coming to an end. Alex was invited to a grand dinner in honour of Sir George Brown of Linkwood, Elgin, Commander of the Light Division, who had been wounded at Inkermann. The guest list came to three hundred, among them distinguished men from further afield than Elgin. What a headache there had been about precedence and seating. When the grace was said and the assembly was seated, the Provost breathed a sigh of relief. Excellent food and excellent service, and surely interesting conversation. It came to the time for the Royal Toast; which was proposed and drunk with fervour. Cigars were lit and the port circulated. Provost Grant rose to make his speech, and was surprised by the entry of a messenger who handed him a telegraphic communication. The Provost began: "Your Royal Highness, my Lords, Gentlemen, perhaps nothing could be more fitting to this auspicious occasion than the message which has just been handed to me, a message of the utmost importance to one and all. Sebastopol has fallen, the Russians have evacuated the south side of the town."

A great shout went up, a spontaneous cheer rang out, and another and another. It happened that among the waiters was a man whose son was at the scene of the battle. What anxiety he had suffered, and what a moment of hope and joy this was! But the war dragged on through the winter and peace did not come until the end of April 1856.

Alex's younger brother Frank, who had worked at *The Courant* for some time, had left to float the *Banffshire Journal*. He eventually returned to Elgin and set up a bookshop. This was a success and enabled him to fulfil a dream he had cherished for some time: he had enough money to rent a farm. The one he chose was Craigfield, which lies to the west and slightly north of Forres, on flat land bounded by the Findhorn and Muckle Burn. [I went to see it – a neat whitewashed, unadorned house with long regular windows letting in the sun from the south. There is a small garden all round it, and the farm buildings are at a slight distance away]. When the railway joined Elgin and Inverness, Craigfield was not too isolated as there used to be a ferry at the Broom of Moy. It was a family move; Frank's mother Janet, and his two unmarried sisters, Margaret and Janet (Jessie) were delighted to go with him to this peaceful retreat, and support him in his new venture.

In 1855 Alex was elected ruling elder by the Presbytery, and in May he went to Edinburgh for the General Assembly. He stayed with his cousins, William and Eliza Grieve at 9 Blacket Place. William's brother Robert, his wife Jane and their children lived next door. When Alex worked in Edinburgh the Grieves had been good to him and this was a happy family reunion. Before Alex left he was persuaded to return soon, bringing Keturah, Johnnie and John Young so that they could get to know their cousins and strengthen family ties in the next generation. So before long Alex arranged the Edinburgh visit, which was also to include going on to Peebles and maybe, if time allowed, they would go to Crail.

In the event it was only Keturah and Alex who went, because Johnnie was unwell and John Young unable to take time off school. Alex may have been a bit relieved – Johnnie was a handsome charming little boy, but at times disobedient. He did not respond to 'a firm hand'. Perhaps he missed his mother even more than Keturah did.

Keturah was four and a half; it was her first 'Grand Tour' and was a great success. She was blissfully happy with her cousins at Number 7, Aggie, Rachel, Marshall and their fascinating four-month-old baby brother Annandale, and with Jane, Eliza and Bella at Number 9. Her cousins began to call her 'Tudy', and Alex found that he did not mind. So this became her name from then on. Alex was delighted with his daughter's sweet manners, her dignity and her happiness. At Peebles the visitors were made very welcome, and in her later years Tudy spoke warmly of "Auntie Betty and Uncle Sandy" (unmarried brother and sister of Janet Russell) who now occupied the family house at School Brae. Alex made careful notes of all the local news to convey to his mother on his return. On the way back they stayed briefly at Crail with dear familiar Uncle William. It was lot of travelling for a wee girl, but it was a happy exciting experience. She had made friendships that were to last throughout her life.

I have a note, which Keturah (Tudy) wrote to her Merson grandparents when she was six years old.

Miss K Russell presents
Compmts. To Mr. and Mrs. Merson
And will be very happy
To drink tea with them
On Friday evening at 6 o'clock
and will appear in full ball
costume.

This little joke was characteristic of her. She loved jokes and was a merry little girl. I have a dress that Aunt Mina made for her, and I wonder if she wore it for the occasion. There is a photograph of Tudy's great-granddaughter (my daughter Susan) wearing this dress. Aunt Mina was a superb needlewoman, and in Elgin Museum there are two very large needlepoint pictures she made, of scenes such as are found in tapestries.

A red-letter day in Elgin was the Centenary of Robert Burns. The council proclaimed a holiday with bands, processions, and in the evening an official dinner for the Council members and the gentlemen. After seeing the procession, Alex's children went to the Mersons at 9 North Street, where a party was held. Tudy had practised two songs of the Immortal Bard, and they all took it in turns to entertain the company. Another celebration was the wedding day of Aunt Mina. It had seemed that Jessie, Barbara and Mina were destined to be old maids, but when Mina was twenty-nine Mr Sim, a bank manager from Lossiemouth, fell in love with her. This brought much happiness to the Merson family. The wedding took place at 9 North Street on 21 August 1859. The bride had made a special dress for Tudy. It turned out to be a very long and happy marriage. The couple had no children, so Tudy was especially favoured and loved. Such a close family life was possible in those days, when many lived in the same home town for the whole of their lives. Such was to be the case with my grandmother.

John Young made good progress with his lessons. One day Alex took him to Inverness to visit the Young family grave in Chapelyard. John's grandfather had been Ebenezer Young, a well-known dominie in Inverness. He died in 1789 aged forty-nine. The large recumbent slab is inscribed with several family names. John read out his own father's name 'EDWARD JAMES YOUNG OF INVERNESS, and MOUNT STEWART, SHETTLEWOOD, AND MELROSE ESTATES, JAMAICA'. John Young developed a strong sense of duty, of sympathy for people, of courage and independence. In 1858, when he was fourteen, he went to London to stay with relatives and for two years was in an office in the city. But business life did not appeal to him and he stuck to his boyhood resolve to do something for the welfare of soldiers. In February he was given a post in the Hospital Commissariat Branch of the Army. His first posting was to Edinburgh, which pleased him and his Elgin family. He continued to come home when on leave and on one of these occasions was involved in an unexpected event.

Alexander Russell with his children, Keturah (Tudy) and Johnnie

CHART D: ABBREVIATED CHART OF FAMILY OF
ALEXANDER RUSSELL, ELGIN

Alexander Russell 1813-1878 fourth son of John Russel, merchant in Elgin and Janet Russell, daughter of Thomas Russell and Margaret Grieve, Peebles (Chart B, Chapter 1)

m. (1) 12.8.1950 Keturah Gerard Merson b.23.6.1832 d.13.4.1854 ch.

1. Keturah Elizabeth Russell b.26.9.1851 at Elgin m. William Adam (see Chart G, Chapter 9)
2. John Patrick Merson Russell b.13.10.1852
3. Charles William Russell b.25.3.1854 d.20.7.1853

m. (2) 16.7.1861 Mary Jane Hulse b. 31.10.1839 Carnpore, India (widow of Robert Cameron, ch. Helen Hulse Cameron 1853-1854; Henry Charles Cameron 1865-1942) ch:

4. Alexander Russell (Alick) 1862-1941 banker in Elgin m. Margaret Helen Leach (no ch.)
5. Thomas Hulse Russell (Tom) b.10.12.1863 Elgin d.1934; emigrated to New Zealand (see Chart F, Chapter 9)

CHAPTER 5

THE RUSSELLS AT MAYNE HOUSE

Alex enjoyed living at Allarburn Farm, but towards the end of 1859 he made two decisions. He had become weary of the unremitting efforts involved in running *The Courant*, besides his other interests. In 1853 he had been elected to the Town Council and was made a Bailie, and in 1858 Commissioner for the Royal Burghs. So he sold *The Courant* business to James Black who took over in 1860. Alex continued to retain the house he owned at Courant Court. On hearing that Captain Young proposed to leave Mayne House, situated just over a mile to the south of the west end of Elgin, Alex made an agreement with Captain Young to take over the remainder of the lease. It was a bigger farm than Allarburn; there were 330 acres of farmland, of which 250 were arable. The estate lay either side of the Findhorn, which in that area was swift-running and dangerous. The small mansion house had been built by one of the Brodie family in the eighteenth century. When the Earl of Findlater bought the estate from the Brodies, he improved the house and put his commissioner, Mr John Ross, into it. Mr Ross laid out fine gardens, lawns, and shrubberies. The Earl had also set out plantations to improve the rather bleak landscape, a carefully planned mixture of firs, larches, and many varieties of hardwoods. These woods and the ornamental gardens were at their best when Alex took over. The rent for the estate in 1878 was £455 per annum, but may have been less in 1860.

That same year Peter Merson retired from his long teaching career. There was a handsome collection, a testimony of affection and gratitude from his colleagues, friends and the many hundreds of pupils he had taught. So generous was the response that he was able to build a new house for himself and the family – Greyfriars Cottage in Abbey Street. The removal from North Street must have been a daunting task; there was a huge collection of rare books, and stacks of papers, besides some precious antique furniture that came from Stoneywood. Peter was now able to follow his many interests; one of these was astronomy. He purchased a telescope (now in Elgin Museum) and in time gave a series of public lectures on astronomy. His daughter Mina (her full name was Williamina) became interested in astronomy, and in turn his granddaughter Tudy.

The year that Peter Merson retired, there was no Academy ball. It was held the following year, but he was unwell and unable to attend and lead off the reel, as was the custom. But he was delighted at the honour paid to him. A portrait of him, painted by Mr Innes of Edinburgh, was placed at the end of the ballroom, and people thought it was the old man himself, standing holding a snuff box in his hand, and large as life.

Alex's children Tudy and Johnnie relished the new life at Mayne House, and Tudy received callers as if she was the mistress of the house. Alex did his best to prepare her for the shock that was in store. He was to remarry. The lady was Mary Cameron, a widow who was fourteen years younger than he was. She was the daughter of Henry Charles Hulse, a veterinary surgeon in the Indian Army, and of Helen Jack who came from a Lossiemouth family. Her husband, Robert Cameron, had been a London merchant. The wedding of Mary Hulse and Robert Cameron had taken place in 1850 (just two weeks before that of Alex and Keturah Merson). Their first child Helen died when a year old and was buried in Highgate Cemetery. Their son Henry was born in 1856, and was eighteen months old when his father died. So Alex and Mary had each endured tragic losses. One supposes that he had met her when she was staying with her Jack relatives. I have no knowledge of how Tudy and Johnnie reacted to the news, but there is a glimpse of possible difficulties from an incident my granny (Tudy) related to my mother.

Mary Hulse Russell

There was a family picnic at Lossiemouth. Henry Cameron was about five years old. Tudy and Johnnie were swimming in the sea, but Henry refused to join them, and seemed to be afraid. His mother was determined not to spoil him, and tried coaxing, then scolding, and finally lost patience. She picked him up under her arm, strode out into the sea and ducked him under the water. He managed to struggle from her, ran out to the sands and rushed away, screaming and in a panic. This upset Tudy greatly and she never forgot it, and was especially kind to the little boy. It must have upset Alex too. However over the years he had a strong influence on Mary and she softened considerably.

A marriage settlement was drawn up, and the wedding was arranged for 16 July 1861. One thing was decided on Mary's wish, that when Alex died he would not be buried in the cathedral in the grave of his beautiful Keturah, but in a new family grave in Elgin Cemetery. Not long before the wedding day a difficulty arose. John Young wrote to say that his leave was due and he would like to come home to Main House. (Alex preferred this name to Mayne.) The dates he gave were those for which bookings had been made for the honeymoon in Paris. There seems to have been no difficulty in sorting this out; it was agreed that John should come with them! Alex's first bride had come home to a ready-made son; his second bride seems to have been equally agreeable about John Young.

The first excitement on the return from the honeymoon was the hearing of the Lossiebank case. The affair began when certain landowners erected fences, and then walls, down to the edge of the river, thus closing an ancient right of way. Alex had written a forthright editorial at the start of the trouble and was at the forefront of the fight. The council was sympathetic but afraid of the expenses of litigation. The citizens held meetings in the Corn Market Hall, which resounded with their indignation, their anger, their resolution and their cheers. Alex was treasurer of the fund-raising committee they set up; it met with universal response and in February a deputation met the council and plans were discussed. It appeared that the council was willing to go to law provided that the public fund proved adequate.

The new editor of *The Courant* took up the matter with vigour: "Paradise Walk closed to the Public", "Landlords asserting their intentions to keep property private", "Unthinkable, outrageous, unjust and illegal". Here is an excerpt from a description of a meeting of the council:

> Messrs Bowie, Stewart and Taylor speak clear, but others are like windmills in the fog or Jack o' Lanterns appearing here there and everywhere, making darkness visible. Dr Geddes' sketch was interesting, Bailie Urquhart's a tub out to catch a whale, the bait as plain as a pikestaff, but nobody would take it. The hook was busked by the leading stars on the opposition bench, and fine feathers gathered some of the magistracy, but the most skilful angling would not do, the Right-of-Way party too old sparrows to be taken by chaff. Twaddle was spoken without mercy. The horrible expense was the cuckoo song of the whole evening.

But eventually the fund-raising was declared to be a success and the council took the case to court. Alex was back from Paris in time to attend the hearing. He must have relished it. A hundred and twenty witnesses were called and he knew every one of them. An exhausted jury had little difficulty in following the summing-up of the Judge, and in reaching a verdict. The editor of *The Courant* was already wording his editorial as he hurried back to the office: "We began the fight. What newspaper has assisted in this battle? Not one. We have stood alone. We kindled the smoke, we fanned the flame, burning down hedges and palings, making dykes crack and tumble beneath it."

Our zestful reporter wrote:

> Victory for the Council. Victory for the citizens of Elgin, old folk, young folk, loons and quines, bairns and all, for their claim to the right to use the walk from Brewery Bridge to Hangman's Ford was vindicated. Outside in the High Street the jubilant noise might ascend from the high dome of St Giles and spin up to the heavens above, to take the good tidings to departed citizens, folk who loved to stroll along Paradise Walk and who, as children, had swum the Lossie Waters from those banks.

So the church bells rang out. It was a good start for Alex and Mary when they returned from their honeymoon. Aunt Margaret had been staying to look after the children, and Alex and the children drove her back to Craigfield next day. They were all in high spirits. Granny Russell was keeping better, and the future seemed bright.

Frank (Alex's brother) began the harvest on 23 August 1861. The following evening, a Friday, he walked from Craigfield to Forres, taking the ferry at the Broom of Moy. He transacted some business; his last call was at the ironmonger's where he wrote some letters and posted them. It was half past nine when he turned for home and met Mr Sclanders, a writer in Forres. They exchanged a few words and Mr Sclanders went on his way, puzzled by something strange in Frank's manner. Frank said that the harvest at Craigfield had started the previous day and "would be finished tomorrow". Mr Sclanders knew the farm and knew that would be impossible.

Frank never got home. Next morning at six o'clock his body was found lying in the shallow water near the Broom of Moy crossing. The ferryman had heard no call the previous evening. Frank's hat and staff had been placed carefully on the bank. It looked as if he had felt ill and gone to the water to get a drink or to cool his face, and had collapsed and drowned. After a terrible weekend of shock and grief at Craigfield there was a post-mortem by two local doctors. They found an abscess above his left eye and "considerable softening of the brain". He had been spared any suffering. That was left to his poor mother and the rest of the family.

There was a large funeral. Frank was laid to rest with his three brothers, but his name was not added to theirs on the tombstone. Alex was too busy, or too disheartened, to see to it. What he did see to was the return of his mother and sisters to Courant Court, the removal and the settlement of all the affairs at Craigfield.

At Main House Mary made preparations for a happy Christmas for the children. But it was a time that was sad and muted for the whole nation. There had been anxiety about the illness of the Prince Consort, but no real fear. The news of his death was a great shock, and the whole nation mourned. Tudy cut out a poem by Tennyson, which had appeared in *The Courant*, and put it in her scrapbook.

The Prince Consort
With trembling fingers did we weave
The holly round the Christmas hearth;
A rainy cloud possess'd the earth
And sadly fell our Christmas Eve.

The Christmas of 1862 was entirely different, for by now there were four children at Main. Alick Russell was born in May 1862, and this seemed to bring cheer to everyone. He was an easy obedient child and his mother softened in her attitude to the young ones. Eighteen months later another baby son arrived and was baptised Thomas Hulse Russell. From the start Tom seemed to have a strong character. As a little boy, he was fascinated by all that went on at the farm. His great love was for horses, and Alex bought ponies for these little boys when they were old enough. Alick was cautious, but Tom, who was full of fun and adventurous, knew no fear and at times was quite reckless. It was a happy busy household. There were six men and a boy employed as farm workers, and three servants and a dairymaid. There were horses in the stables, but I do not know what sort of conveyance to take the children to school, and to take Mary and Alex to various parties, soirées, dinners and balls. Did Alex buy a 'sociable' with a

The Russell family at Main House, Elgin, c.1874

removal hood, useful for picnics, which became a family tradition, and also a little pony trap?

In 1863 Alex was unanimously elected to succeed Provost Grant. It was the fiftieth year of his age. There are two portraits of him: in the one commissioned sometime during his six years as Provost, he was fair-haired and clean-shaven. In the later one he has a handsome silver beard. His mother used to say that he was the image of William Chambers, who was a cousin of hers, and there is certainly a strong likeness to the portrait of William Chambers at the Chambers Institute at Peebles. (Alex Russell and William Chambers were both grandsons of David Grieve of Jedderfield).

In July 1865 Alec and Mary had a baby daughter, baptised Mary

Cameron Hulse Russell. There was more rejoicing. But in that year Tudy and Johnnie had to face a big change in their lives. The Elgin Academy had suffered from the results of a long lawsuit. Mr Morrison gave in his notice and set up a private boarding school taking with him some of the best scholars. Before long he had a hundred and twenty pupils and was able to charge four times the fees of the Academy. Alex decided that Johnnie would do better at a boarding school, and for some reason it was settled that he would go to the Madras College at St Andrews. Alex had long intended that Tudy would go to a small boarding school in Edinburgh when she was fourteen. I wonder if one factor in these decisions was that fashion at this time dictated that children of the 'upper classes' should be trained to speak 'good English'? Were Tudy and Johnnie using the vernacular of the farm and house servants?

The Madras College had a fine reputation. It was founded by the handsome legacy from Dr Andrew Bell, who brought a new method of education based on the monitorial system whereby the younger boys were taught by senior ones. The pupils sat in big bays in the large room. In Johnnie's time there were about nine hundred pupils. The school attracted the children of parents from all over Britain and from abroad. The boys boarded at the homes of the masters. Johnnie settled in easily and enjoyed the companionship of new friends. He wrote to his sister Tudy to tell her of his adventures. The Master of the Mathematics was nicknamed 'Billum' and he was a good teacher and popular with the boys, but there was another master who was "a bit free with the tawse". Johnnie had been told of a master who had just left who used to "give palmies all round if anyone so much as smiled". In the evening a student from St Mary's College took coaching sessions for Johnnie and a few others.

Saturday was a half-holiday and Johnnie and his friends walked along the cliffs to the Maiden Rock and climbed it, and then went on to the Rock and Spindle. On their return they had a treat – two mutton pies apiece, and then the older boys told some tales around the fire. St Andrews was a place of ghosts. The White Lady lived in a tower

Alexander Russell   *William Chambers*

in the cathedral wall. There was a dog that walked high above the ground at Deans Court. And Archbishop Sharp's phantom coach drove down South Street on a certain day of the year. Johnnie hoped he would see all of these ghosts. There were tales of the wild capers of the students when they dressed up for Kate Kennedy day. There were lots of school stories too – of Ochter Lony (*sic*) who climbed up the ruins of Blackfriars Chapel (on the South Street side of Madras), got stuck and had to be rescued, and of another boy who ate so many of Mrs McKenzie's (Bell Street) soda scones that he died of an explosion in his stomach!

Tudy was booked to attend 'Miss Balmain's Establishment for the Education of Young Ladies' at Great King Street, Edinburgh, in September 1865. But the boarding house was at 14 Heriot Row (and maybe the school in its earlier days). The advertisement ran:

> The whole arrangements and studies are under the personal supervision of Miss Balmain, whose long experience in the education of Young Ladies fully qualifies her to meet the

expectations of those parents and guardians who may entrust their Daughters or Wards to her care. The number of young ladies received as boarders being very limited, the most careful attention is paid to each in regard to health, moral and religious training, the preparation of studies, and their comfort in every respect. The first masters attend to give instruction in all the branches of a thorough education and accomplishments, and Miss Balmain is assisted by Foreign and English Governesses. French and German conversation daily.

When preparations were being made for Tudy to go away to school, there was an altercation between her and her stepmother. Mary had found a trunk in the attic containing dresses which had belonged to Tudy's dear, dead mama, and had conceived the idea that some of these might be 'made down' by a dressmaker. Tudy was strongly against this. A compromise had to be made; one new dress was made and three were altered. My grandmother told my mother that she felt a freak and avoided wearing them. However, she had many advantages when she began school in Edinburgh. She benefited from the music and the dancing lessons she had enjoyed at Elgin, and was well versed in most subjects. I have her book of essays and this is an extract from one on 'Memory'. "A tree, a rock, may recall the scene of a happy childhood, when all was fair and bright, and no cares had come to oppress. Far from home and among strangers every object is brought before the mind's eye, it may be by seeing a familiar face in the street. Thus living pictures are constantly brought to mind! How dejected and miserable we would be if we had no memory." The following is from an essay on 'Winter':

"The year is now drawing to a close, but we all look forward with delight to the coming Christmas, especially girls at school who long for home and holidays." From another essay headed "My Studies" we learn "I am studying at present History, Geography, Grammar, Composition, Etymology, Literature, Arithmetic, Writing, Music, Singing, Dancing, French, German, and Natural Philosophy. I like them all very much with the exception of Arithmetic, Morell's Grammar and Natural Philosophy. Music is a delight. If only there were more time to practise! I am very fond of drawing and water colour painting. Our Perspective is not so interesting, but we intend some Saturday soon to take a run into the country and sketch from Nature."

The young ladies were taken to concerts, and on Saturday afternoons to hear stirring music played in the Princes Street Gardens by the band of the King's Own Regiment. The church the pupils attended was St Stephen's where the Minister, Dr Muir, was strongly opposed to the Innovations. Tudy's father, a moderate in all things, was strongly in favour of them. Mr and Mrs Stevenson and their son Robert Louis Stevenson lived next door but one to Miss Balmain's, and on at least one occasion the girls assisted at a bazaar held by Mrs Stevenson in her house. Besides seeing a deal of her Grieve cousins, Tudy made lifelong friends at school. Her 'best friends' were Nellie Rich from London, Penny Trotter and 'Henry' (Henrietta) Hall. Henry married the minister at Dornoch, and she and Tudy visited each other regularly until they were well into their eighties.

The Christmas holidays of 1865 reunited the family, and Tudy became an expert in looking after her little sister. I suppose it reflects the Victorian way of life that I have to write so much of untimely deaths. In March Alex was obliged to sit down and write a letter to Tudy to break the news that her baby sister had died, and to exhort her to be as brave as the baby's mother was. Tudy felt a deep sympathy for Mary, and this drew them closer together. It had brought such happiness for Mary to have another little girl, a solace for the daughter she had lost. And Tudy shows some of her feelings in an essay she wrote entitled 'Youth': "When you are young, all is sweet and calm and sparkling as it were a thousand diamonds. But Youth is but an empty dream. 'Tis a pity the gilding wears off so soon. In Youth little clouds may come but soon they pass away and give place to the greater cares and trials of life."

Tudy had always been close to her Merson grandparents. She and Johnnie were their only grandchildren. On the Russell side of the family John and Janet had just three grandchildren, Tudy, Johnnie and Jessie, the daughter of Alex's oldest brother Thomas. In December

1860 Jessie married Franc Conquergood of Leith, and in the following years they had a family of six children. [Here I must relate a strange coincidence, the sort of thing that sometimes happens to amateur genealogists. In 1980 I was in Edinburgh, sitting in Register House, waiting in the queue for the moment when a certain door would open, and we would secure our tickers for a day's search. An elderly lady came in and sat down beside me. I asked her which family she was researching. "I'm up from Eastbourne," she said. "It's an unusual name – a family from Leith called Conquergood." I was electrified, and said that we had that name in out Russell tree. Just who WAS she? "My grandfather was the Franc Conquergood of Leith. He married a Jessie Russell from Elgin. My mother was their daughter Isobel, and my father was Henry Charles Cameron." I could scarcely believe it. "But that was the name of my granny's step-brother," I told her. "That's right," she said. "Keturah Russell's father married for a second time – to Mary Cameron." I thought for a bit, and then said, "So what relation are you and I to each other?" She was stumped. We both began to laugh, and arranged to have lunch together. The next year I visited her in Eastbourne.]

In the summer of 1866 the Mersons were very cheered by a visit from their son Charles. He had been the collegiate minister at Arbroath for twenty years and then he took up the post of colonial chaplain at St Andrew's, Columbo, Ceylon. In many ways Charles was like his father; at Aberdeen University (where he went as a student at thirteen years old) he proved to be a first class mathematician. He was a winning and affable man, popular and with a good sense of humour. He was also an accomplished musician. Charles had come home to Elgin at regular intervals. This time he had good news, he was soon to be married and to bring his bride home on his next visit. He found his father in a poor way, scarcely able to walk, but admirable in spirit and taking great pleasure in his books and his many visitors.

Christmas 1867 was a sad time for the Russells and the Mersons. On 22 December Mary and Alex went to the Academy Ball, having first looked in to see Alex's parents. That night Peter Merson died peacefully in his sleep; it seemed a fitting time for his going. *The Courant* gave prominence to his obituary. Here is an extract from much that was said in his praise: "In fancy we see him standing in the street, staff in hand, in the middle of a group of grey-haired men who were once boys at his school. If told of a death or a misfortune being the lot of any of his pupils, he felt a father to them, his big heart swelling with sorrow for their miseries."

I am told there are scores of papers relating to Peter Merson in the archives at Elgin. Someone wrote these simple lines about him:

> *Though small of stature, of Stentorian voice,*
> *Of wit a fund, of words a countless choice,*
> *In learning he was varied and profound,*
> *In truth intrepid, in religion sound.*
> *In controversy seldom known to spare,*
> *But humble as a Publican in prayer.*
> *And tho' such manners strange, of feeling mind,*
> *Such Merson was, with justice vain.*
> *Oh, when shall Elgin see his like again?*

The Merson tombstone is on the outside wall at the east end of the cathedral. The words relating to Peter are THE MEMORY OF THE JUST IS BLESSED. I like to think of his courage in sticking to what he thought was right. He was a man of integrity.

Tudy wrote an essay on "Old Age" in which she compared old age with a glorious sunset.

> When we see the darkness creeping on, we do not give way to grief, for we know that the day will dawn again. So it is with Death. The bustle and the anxieties of life have become distasteful to the old man. His mind is calm and peaceful. The aged Christian feels himself growing weaker and weaker, and at last when the Angel of Death comes stealthily upon him, he bows his head and gives up the ghost.

Her faith remained strong, but sometimes awkward questions arose. When she was ninety years old she said to my mother, "I've been wondering, Mary – when I join my young mama in Heaven – and I hope I shall – won't she find it rather strange that I am an old lady and I was a little girl of three when she left me?" My mother was very good at answering questions but I can't think what her reply to that one might have been.

CHAPTER 6

PROVOST RUSSELL

The scene is Elgin, the time is Christmas 1868, the place the Assembly Rooms, the occasion the concert of the Choral Society. There was a pleasant hum as friends greeted friends and exchanged news. Whispered comments were made when it was noticed that two young ladies were wearing 'the bustle'- a new departure in fashion. The party from Main House had arrived in good time, all seven of them, Provost and Mrs Russell, Miss Keturah, Tom, Alick and John Young. John was home on leave from the Abyssinian campaign and had received high praise for his part in it. He had been given promotion, and had hopes of meeting Miss Nightingale.

With the choir seated there was an expectant hush, and on the entry of Herr Noah a burst of applause. He bowed, turned, raised his baton and then came forth the stirring strains of Handel's 'Lift up your heads, Oh ye gates'. One treat followed another: 'The March of the Men of Harlech', "O'er the Green and Sparkling Waters', 'Weel May the Keel Row', and 'Ye Banks and Braes o' Bonny Doon'. Finally the Honourable Mrs Norton gave her interpretation of 'Absalom'. It brought round upon round of applause. Tudy had attended some fine concerts in Edinburgh, but many years later she remembered this one with joy, as one of the happiest family occasions.

We now turn to consider Alex as Provost of Elgin. He was indefatigable; he seemed scarcely to take a break in the round of meetings and the aftermath, preparations and more meetings. A special meeting of the council was called over the General Police and Improvements Act. Alex knew that somehow he had to reason, to push them and coax them into accepting it. He began by sketching the state of Elgin forty years ago, and contrasting it with the present happy position. He continued: "It is, however, a curious fact that when any public improvement is proposed, there always has been, and I suppose always will be, some objectors. I am told that when gas was being introduced some parties actually denounced it as the devil's light, from its being conveyed in underground pipes, and would have nothing to do with it. I was personally cognisant of the strong opposition that was got up to the introduction of water, the most valuable and successful of improvements, so far as the health and comfort of the inhabitants are concerned, that has ever been effected in Elgin.

"But I suppose there are grumblers in every community, and so we are not singular, and must be content to bear with them. Even in the present case where the subject is one in which the prosperity of the town, as well as the health of its inhabitants, is deeply involved, I regret to learn that its adoption is to be opposed on the grounds that it should be determined by the ratepayers and not by the police. But the ratepayers have been duly consulted."

Alex won the day, as he had on previous occasions. At the beginning of his second term of office his foremost task was to deal with the aftermath of the Academy Case Appeal. As a result of it the council was seriously in debt. "There is a gap and the two ends must be brought to meet," he declared. It was not a policy to make a man popular. The split between the members of the Established Church and the Non-conformists caused bitterness and a divisiveness that lasted even after the lifetime of the protagonists. On one matter Alex was firm. He declared, "The Academy has always been a pet object of mine, and for this reason: that without a good Liberal education at a cheap rate such a city as Elgin would not prosper." He had proposed that a subscription fund for a new school should be started, and had laid down £25 from his own pocket, but the scheme was not feasible without a contribution from the impoverished council. So Alex set to work and had estimates made for repairs and renovations of the old buildings (most of which, in the event, was done for him without cost) and when they had agreed on the plans he opened up a subscription list. He supervised the work, and the fund-raising covered the whole cost. (In 1886 a new Academy was built in Moray Street).

Alex was also a director of Anderson's Institution, took a great interest in its management and the welfare of its inmates, and spent a lot of his working time there. He was deeply involved in plans for building a new Morayshire Poorhouse. It was sad that so many hopes, so much effort and goodwill and so much money went into a scheme that was never really successful. 'The design of the building indicates that those who planned it did not appreciate the feelings of those who were to live there. It was designed as a Grand Institution, where rigid administration, a rule of cleanliness (as next to Godliness) and a strict segregation of the sexes (to ensure absolute morality) worked against the real human needs. The prevailing ethos - that there was stigma in failure to conform, and that there were two classes of poor people, the "respectable poor" and the "undeserving poor"- led to a lack of true understanding. Many of those who were forced to go "inside" lost their sense of pride; families and friends were split up, and in spite of a high standard of cleanliness and the grandiose surroundings, it was a sad and unnatural life.

The Morayshire Combination Poorhouse was erected at Bishopmill, Elgin, on 2 June 1865. The building was impressively large, of the 'Strawberry Gothic' type. The main block was two-storeyed; in the centre was the Porter's Lodge, with massive iron gates, and wings on either side, which were cut by transepts. There were several separate departments in the dayrooms (actually called drawing rooms!) on the ground floor. The dormitories were above. The Probationary and Vagrant wards were by the Porter's Lodge. There was a secure provision for lunatic paupers, and other separate ones for men, for women, for boys and for girls. Each had its own 'airing yard' behind the main building and in front of a single-storey building, which ran right along the back and was for offices. The impression was "of a wilderness of rooms". The Governor's apartment was on the first floor and centrally placed. To complete the building a high wall ran right round the precinct, blocking out the fine view from the ground floor windows.

It was the dread of many poor folk that they would end up in the Poorhouse. Robert Young wrote in his *Annals of Elgin* (1878), "The Poorhouse was built to hold about 150 inmates, and although it is clean and comfortable, it is only half full. It is doubtful whether the inmates have the same enjoyment as when they wandered through the country asking for alms and victuals and returning to their miserable homes at night." The Poorhouse was taken down in 1974; all that remains of it is a piece of the old outside wall. In its place is Bishopmill House, a modern Home for old people. It was opened in November 1975; a greater contrast in appearance and character cannot be imagined.

[Digressing into the future to my own childhood, in the year 1925 at nine years old I was sent to a primary school in Bishop Auckland to prepare for the 11+ exam. This school had a good educational record. Nearby was the Workhouse, a formidable building. A group of girls from the Workhouse attended this school and were in our class. We all felt very sorry for them. They were set apart by their hideous ill-fitting uniforms. They seemed to suffer from perpetual colds, and had no hankies, so they wiped their noses on the sleeves of their bulky red jerseys. There was a sewing teacher who nagged at them mercilessly. We were engaged on making paper patterns for knickers with gussets. We each had to cut out the several pieces and pin them onto a square of white cotton material. Most of us lost our way, but none so badly as the poor Workhouse girls. The teacher lost her temper and hit them. I was very upset by this, and my parents removed me at the end of term and sent me to a small private school, an altogether different world. But on my daily way from the bus I passed a slum house with a door that was divided into two horizontal parts. The top part was usually open, and I could see several half-dressed little children in filthy conditions. There were always two or three of them crying. I asked my mother if I could leave them some clothes, and she packed up a parcel. As I drew near

79

the house I was overcome with doubts and embarrassment. I simply slung the parcel over the door and fled at top speed.]

As Provost, Alex was deeply involved with problems which arose at Dr Gray's Hospital. It was – and remains so today – a great asset to Elgin. So well was it thought of that members of the town council found it hard to believe that complaints received about mismanagement could be justified. The murmuring began after a smallpox epidemic in Elgin, which broke out at the end of 1865, and continued into the New Year. Alex was indefatigable about visiting the bereaved families - altogether fifty-three citizens died. Those who were most seriously ill were taken to the top floor of the hospital. Subsequently at a council meeting the comment was made that hardly any of these survived, though it had to be admitted that they were very ill on admittance. Patients with other types of less virulent diseases were taken into the wards, and some voiced the opinion that this seemed inadvisable. There was a full discussion on the complaints that had been lodged. The Provost advised that these should be listed and sent to the Trustees of the hospital, but he was over-ruled. A committee of investigation was set up; it was agreed that the Provost, the Magistrates and three chosen councillors should get to work at once and report back as soon as possible. " We had a pretty hard time of it," Alex said, "We had six nights a week, four or five hours every evening spent on examining families." The committee gathered hundreds of statements made by these families who were concerned about events at the hospital. At the hospital itself they were met with opposition from the House Surgeon. He refused to allow them to enter the wards, or to make entries from the Register of Deaths or from the book of admissions, from which they found that two pages of entries were missing. Nor would he allow them to see the Register of patients expelled and entries for the reasons. Alex was now sure that there was cause for investigation. Legal advice was taken as to the rights of the town council to make this investigation, and an independent investigator was appointed. There was sufficient evidence to dismiss the House Surgeon and the Matron. A new House Surgeon was appointed, an excellent man, and there were no further complaints.

The Lunatic Asylum was a matter of great concern to Alex Russell. A pauper Lunatic Asylum had been built at the back of Dr Gray's Hospital in 1834. It was maintained by annual assessment for support of the fabric, and each parish paid board for its own patients. The passing of the Lunacy Act in 1861 made it necessary for the town council to consider its local provision. "An Account of a Visit to the County Lunatic Asylum" appeared in *The Courant* in 1861, describing the Asylum in critical terms.

It is an L-shaped building, with stairs in the left branch; there are several faults in design. The kitchen is in the wrong place, and there is a want of a proper airing yard. The rooms have small high windows like police cells, and the inmates cannot see out of them. These rooms are high and dark. The floors of the bedrooms are of pavement and so they are damp. The doors of the bedrooms are of solid wood, very heavy, about two and a half inches thick and capable of keeping mad elephants in place instead of men. The dormitories are too crowded and the place is out of date. But it is quiet and orderly, the inmates playing at games of draughts, and some art work. Those who are able work in the fields. A dance is held once a fortnight. What a great change has come since the reign of mercy succeeded the Reign of Terror.

I wonder whether it was Alex who wrote this article? There were discussions at council meetings on various occasions. One suggestion was that there might be set up separate units for (1) pauper lunatics, (2) for the curable and (3) for the incurable. Eventually Alex gave his opinion. "You cannot define insanity cases are alike. The estimate is that it would cost £45 for an incurable and £32 for a pauper lunatic. There would be inferior asylums, and these are people who are labouring under the greatest of human calamities. We trust our deep sympathy for them will not wax cold, though the opulent may grumble to give them food and shelter in the asylum. For many inmates the asylum was a hospital for curing illness, and only a small number of patients are excited and dangerous and in need of a different sort of care".

At length it was decided to replace the present Asylum with a new building on the same site, and also that further provision would be made for farm work and for gardening. The outdoor work, in particular work with animals such as pigs, proved to be a great boon to many of the patients. [All this puts me in mind of Stratheden Hospital at Cupar, Fife, where I worked from 1966–1969 at Playfair House, a residential unit for disturbed children, which was a part of the hospital. It was during my time there that the farm and the garden where some of the residents worked were closed down on the grounds that it was unprofitable. Many years later, in spite of its successes, Playfair House as a residential unit was closed, and in the course of time several wards in the main hospital have been closed down.]

It was the constant burden on the Provost to keep to the fore the aim of balancing the budget, and in 1865 the outbreak of foot-and-mouth disease on some Morayshire farms and a ban on holding markets for some months. This meant a loss to the council. Penny paring was more difficult than large gestures. Yet steadily Alex had his way and saw things coming right for the council's finances. His second term of office as Provost was to end in November 1869, and although there was a good deal of lobbying to persuade him to continue, he was firm in his resolution to retire. It was recognised that the town had the services of a first-class businessman with the mind of a lawyer. He had dealt with the transfer of land for building, much of it held by the Guildry. As Provost he was an ex-officio director of Lossiemouth Harbour Board, and there was a heavy demand for money for repairs to the harbour. The money was found. Alex was only fifty-six but he realised that it was taking too much of a toll on him. However he agreed to continue as a council member. His dearest daughter had now left school and was at home helping her mother. Alex wanted to spend more time with his family. In particular he felt that he needed to give more assistance to Mrs Merson. In the early summer she had received troubling reports from Colombo about their son Charles; his wife wrote to say that he had been running a fever intermittently. He had been given a year's leave so that they might come back to Elgin and he would recover his strength. In June the devastating news arrived that he had died. In spite of the sadness which this tragic news brought to the family, and other burdens and anxieties, the family at Main was fortunate. The young people were by disposition cheerful, hard at work, and with many friends.

Alex made his leave-taking speech as Provost with a summary of the improved financial situation of the Council. It gave him great pleasure to announce a pleasant surprise. "I have to hand a cheque from Mr Brander for erecting a new bridge over the Lossie at Marywell, as a mark of confidence in me and approval of my conduct as Lord Provost of Elgin. I have to thank you and bid you respectfully adieu." Nevertheless, he continued as a member of the council until late in 1872.

CHAPTER 7

MISS K.E. RUSSELL

And so in July 1869 Tudy Russell's schooldays came to an end. Miss Balmain was somewhat progressive and the girls were given an excellent education. Tudy's favourite authors were Sir Walter Scott and Charles Dickens. It had been a red-letter day when Mr Dickens came to Edinburgh to give a public reading from some of his works. Tudy and her friends were delighted; however she wrote in her letter home, "Miss Balmain and some of the mistresses did not approve of his elocution. They remarked that his pronunciation of English was regrettable." For her school prizes Tudy received a complete leather-bound set of the *Works of Charles Dickens*. These she cherished, and she read her favourites many times.

Was being grown-up a sad anti-climax? Her 'Coming-out' took place at the Masonic Ball, but she left no record of her feelings about it. Her work at home seems to have been helping her young brothers with their homework, helping 'mama' by doing certain chores in the house, practising her music, and sketching. Although there were highlights in Elgin's social life (she greatly enjoyed the parties), I think that she wished for a measure of independence. After Johnnie left school he began his training with legal firm in Elgin. No University days for him, and it was about fifty years too soon for any such opportunity for Tudy. She worked hard at her music and her art: in July 1871 she had a short holiday in the Lake District, and I have her sketch-book from that time.

In 1871 Alex accepted an invitation to become joint agent to the Royal Bank with the firm of Murdoch and Forsyth. There was a carefully worded agreement, which included a clause that his sons would have the option of being employees of the Elgin branch of the Royal Bank. As for John Young, in 1870 his career began as an organiser, and then as administrator-in-chief, of Red Cross work. In that year the British Red Cross Society was formed, with generous subscriptions from the public to be applied to the relief of the sick and wounded in the Franco-German war. John Young, aged twenty-seven, was placed at its disposal by the Secretary of State for War to organise the equipment being furnished by the Royal Arsenal Woolwich. It was all arranged in ten days, and John travelled to Le Havre with army surgeons and Hospital Corps. He took the first convoy of fresh supplies into Paris on the conclusion of the Armistice. For his services he was decorated by the French Government. He returned to Woolwich as Control Officer and was soon appointed as Commissariat in Charge of all troops. He had a long and honourable career, motivated by his admiration for and friendship with Florence Nightingale, was awarded several medals and in 1907 a knighthood.

Now we return to August 1872. Johnnie had a friend in Elgin, who through a mutual acquaintance knew a Mr. William Alves. He was an agent of the Royal Bank in Edinburgh, so he sometimes came to Elgin on bank business, and in the course of things met Mr Alexander Russell. It seemed inevitable that Mr Alves and Miss Russell would meet. Each was favourably impressed.

It was a social season at Main. Nellie Rich, a friend of Tudy from their schooldays, had come north for a holiday from her home in London. She was accompanied by her fiancé, Fred Hamilton, who had relatives in the area. I have a small leather-bound diary kept by Tudy. It begins with the entry regarding presents sent to her by Mr Alves.

1872 K.E. Russell August 1872

Wednesday, August 28th 1872. Drove into town and met Papa. Received presents of eleven pieces of music, this diary, and Confessions. Hamie and Nellie came. Turtle doves. Marshall Grieve dined with us. Mama finished her crinoline!!!!

85

[The exclamation marks were no doubt because the crinoline was now outmoded. From a book by Bethia Walford *Recollections of a Scottish Novelist:* "We were wedged together in carriages, and hoops billowed up to the roof; we scuttled crab-like through turn-stiles; we were unable to pass in gangways; we endured every imaginable form of inconvenience and heard ourselves derided by fathers, husbands and brothers, and we boldly faced them, vowing that come what might, we would never, never give up the crinoline."]

Tudy recorded that she had written to thank Mr Alves for the presents mentioned above, on that day mama, and on another day papa, received letters from Mr Alves. Of the diary entries which followed some are longer, others are brief and mundane, such as: "Sewing all day"; "Made plum jam"; "Drove into Elgin, called on Grandmama Merson and on Grandmama Russell."

> Sunday, September 8th 1872. Morning church, Mr. Mackie preached from 1st John v.4 'Faith'. Afternoon, Mr Cooper Hebrews X11 v. 29 'Consuming Fire'. Walked to the Cemetery after dinner. After tea, music and talking, prayers and supper.

> Friday, Septr 6th 1872. Red Letter day. Went with Andrew Haig to Mrs Forsyth's. Mr.Alves there. Went to the Railway Station and got a nice sight of the Queen. Very pleasant and happy looking. She gave me a familiar nod!!!

The Queen was travelling from Balmoral Castle to Dunrobin Castle, and had agreed to stop at Elgin Station. From a detailed account in *The Courant*:

> The triumphant arch of greenery and blossoms in red, white and blue was a splendid idea. Hanging baskets echoed the colours, flag and pennants stirring in the gentle breeze. A new red carpet awaited blessing of regal feet. What an occasion! (It was said that the last time a reigning monarch visited Elgin it was the ill-fated Mary Queen of Scots.
> The Provost and dignitaries made an impressive entry. And with them came the Duke of Gordon and the Earl of March. And then - a gentle pulse in the air, the rhythm of metal on metal, the

throb of steam like a great heart-beat, and the splendid shining powerful creature loomed, bore in, came to an obedient halt. The Stationmaster stepped forward, bowing deeply as he opened the door. Lord Granville stepped out then and handed down Her Majesty, and a great cheer went up from one and all, followed by an instant freezing to attention as the Regimental Band struck up the National Anthem.

The Queen stayed for about a quarter of an hour, and the article lists those to whom she spoke. It happened that Alex and Mary missed this event as they were now away on holiday at Bridge of Allan. Tudy was keeping house with frequent visits from Auntie Margaret. These are few more entries selected from her diary.

August 31st. Aunt Margaret came at 10 a.m. Young man came to teach us the sewing machine. Very apt pupils. Got through a lot of work. Rained very much all day. Harvest begun but obliged to stop. Administered poison to the rats.

Tuesday, Septr. 3rd. Busy sewing. Rain, Rain, Rain. John and Henry came home drenched. Made up butter. Papa wrote to Mr Alves. Met Andrew Haig at the station on the 3.15 from Aberdeen. Drove out together. Music in the evening.

September 5th.. Busy all day making dresses for the London trip. Andrew Haig drove to Pluscarden and back. Got six beautiful songs from Mr. Alves.

Septr.15th. Very busy preparing for party on Thursday. Telegram from Mama telling me to go by all means. Letter from Aggie Grieve wishing me to go to Edinburgh Saturday and then to Strone on 23rd. I write to Papa and Mama to ask their permission - like a dutiful child.

Thursday, Septr. 17th. Drove to Braelossie to party at 8 o'clock. Enjoyed myself so much. Delightful party. Went to supper with Willie Ross.

Friday, Septr.20th Heard from Papa and Mama they allow me to go to Edinburgh on Saturday. They will be home 2.29.

Saturday, Septr. 21st Went to party at Ladyhill. Splendid party. Went to supper with Dr Sanderson. Went home at 2.a.m and finished packing. Went to bed tired at 4.a.m.

In the diary is a careful list of Tudy's holiday plans; without doubt there was a copy for mama and papa.

September 21st to September 23rd At Salisbury View, Edinburgh.

September 23rd to October 1st At Strone, Argyllshire.

October 1st to October 4th At 7, Blacket Place, Edinburgh.

October 5th to November 22 At 1, Eagle Place, London.

November 22nd to December 14th At 7, Blacket Place, Edinburgh .

December 14 to January 2nd At Salisbury View, Edinburgh.

The Edinburgh Grieve families were very much part of my grandmother's family life. So here I must digress to recount briefly some of the story of some members of this remarkable family who were close to my Elgin Russells. Robert Chambers wrote of the sons of David Grieve of Jedderfield, Peebles: "most of them floated on their own merits to much superior positions. This family afforded an example of the virtuous frugal life of the rural economy of Scotland previous to that extension of industry which brought wealth and comforts our country."

Robert Grieve was born in November 1776 at Jedderfield, He was the youngest – the fourteenth child of David Grieve. For a short time he worked on his father's farm, but then left for Glasgow with only a bag of tools to serve him. He fell in love with Agnes Symington of Romano Bridge. Her father intended her to marry an older man, a prosperous merchant in Peebles. But early one morning Agnes climbed down from her bedroom window, mounted pillion on Robert Grieve's horse, and they rode off. It was a very happy marriage. Robert set up a successful business in Edinburgh at 76–77 South Bridge. He had a large warehouse for "carpets, beds, printed damasks and linens". Later the business moved to 83 George Street. By 1841 the Grieves were living at 2 St John's Hill beside the Queens Park. They had three sons and five daughters, but lost three of these children in childhood.

In 1846 Robert retired and the family moved to a fashionable new suburb of Edinburgh. He bought 9 Blacket Place, a house built to his design by his brother Archibald Grieve, who was a builder in Stirling. This house was part of a new estate given over to large-scale development for private houses; many were built in the Greek classical style. Security and privacy were given to Blacket Place by means of gates that were closed at dusk.

Robert and Agnes' oldest son was named David after his grandfather Grieve. His interests lay in geology and in 1828 he became a fellow of the Royal Physical Society of Edinburgh; over the years he contributed many papers to its Proceedings. His work took him to various ports in England, but when he retired he settled in Edinburgh and became President of the Society. His address on his presidential leave-taking, the one hundred and seventh session of the Society, was "A general enquiry and review into the progress of science during the last fifty years". It is well worth reading.

The second son of Robert and Agnes was named Robert Symington Grieve. There was a close relationship between father and son, as young Robert worked in the family business. In 1841 he married Jane Sommerville, a daughter of William Sommerville and Jane Ferguson of Laurencekirk Cottage, Glencorse. William Sommerville founded the Dalmore Mill at Penicuik; part of his story is to be found in *The Last Mill on the Esk* by Nigel Watson 1987. [Oh what serendipity for me in my search! I got in touch with the author and in turn was given names and addresses of descendants of the Grieves. Robbie and Jean Bartholomew have been good and helpful 'cousins' and friends to me. Jean's grandfather was Symington Grieve.]

Robert and Jane Grieve lived at 25 Upper Grey Street, Edinburgh, but in 1846 they moved to 7 Blacket Place, next door to Robert's father, who had for some time been a widower. He was no doubt delighted to have an increasing number of grandchildren so near. When the old man died in 1853 his third son William, with his wife Eliza Sommerville and their children, moved into his father's house.

Eliza was a sister of Jane. In the course of time Robert and Jane had eight children and William and Eliza had nine. What fun, what parties, what outings to come! The future seemed bright.

But in August 1862 disaster struck. William (then forty years old) died as the result of a tragic accident. Herbert, the youngest child, was sixteen months old and Eliza was expecting another baby. William had bought land and made plans for the building of a larger house, just outside the east end of Blacket Place, at 64 Dalkeith Road. After the new baby was born Eliza and the children moved into the new house named Salisbury View. The baby was baptised William, but he died of scarlet fever when he was three and a half. Running ahead of my main story I found it comforting to know that this was a happy household. The children adored their mother, who was a kind and loving woman. Four of the children, Harold, Herbert, Bertie and Amy, continued to live at home. Their mother Eliza was an invalid for some years, and was tenderly cared for until her death in 1901.

Two of William and Eliza's sons, Symington and Sommerville Grieve, were both in the wine business, but also became well known in Edinburgh circles through their contributions to various journals. Symington was an ornithologist, a botanist and an archaeologist. He became à Fellow of the Royal Physical Society in 1886.

In October 1882 Symington Grieve married Christian, the daughter of a carpet merchant John Anderson and his wife Jane Marshall. Symington and his wife were great travellers. They went to New Zealand in 1894. One day Symington went off to climb a mountain near Lake Wakatipu. He wrote: "A dreadful storm of wind and rain came over and I decided to turn for home. Just then an elderly man approached, heavily laden with botanical specimens, and I offered to carry some of his burden." Symington soon learned that his companion was James Dall, the well-known naturalist. They talked for some time about the kiwi. Dall sent off to Edinburgh a collection of skins, skeletons and eggs of the kiwi, and Symington gifted these to the Chambers Street Museum.

On an expedition to the mountainous islands of Dominica in the British West Indies, Symington studied the capped petrel, and also a strange horned beetle, the *Passulius unicornus*, and subsequently wrote papers on these subjects. But his greatest love and the driving interest in his life was the study of the archaeology and folklore of the western islands of Colonsay and Oronsay Two handsome volumes, the result of forty-five years of research, are the products of his annual visits to these islands. The volumes have the following: "These pages are inscribed to my beloved wife who has encouraged my studies and joined with me in the joys and hardships of travels in many lands."

Symington and Christian moved from one pleasant house in Newington to another. Their last home was at 11 Lauder Road. They had only one son William, and they suffered the heartbreak of his accidental death when he was twenty-one years old. Their three daughters shared their interests and one of them, Jean, became a fellow of the Royal Physical Society. When Symington died in 1932, aged eighty-two, the family had an unbroken membership of the R.P.S. for 104 years. The other daughters, Edith and Marjorie, 'Miggs', both married and there are descendants in Scotland and New Zealand.

Symington and his brother Sommerville shared the same interests. Sommerville married Mary Buntin Macleod and they eventually settled at 1 Queen's Terrace. They had a son, Angus, and two daughters. Angus had a distinguished career during and after the Great War. In 1928 when he was Vice-President of the High Court of Jerusalem, he fell ill and died, leaving a wife and young children. Sommerville held various public offices in Edinburgh. He was an Assistant of the Edinburgh Trade Protection Society, an Assistant of the Edinburgh Merchant Company and Vice-Convenor of Daniel Stewart's College. He died after a long illness on 23 January 1932, a month before the death of his brother Symington.

Returning to Tudy's holiday: her diary is fairly detailed, and I have made extracts from her day-by-day entries. I have selected some, which relate to her friends and family, some from what is almost a list of the London sightseeing expeditions (leaving out the careful notes she made), and some which describe her feelings about the concerts and theatres and parties. The contrast between the two Edinburgh Grieve households and that of the Rich family is notable. Mr and Mrs Rich kept the young people entertained - Tudy, Nellie, her younger sister and brother, Katy and Harry, and Mr Fred Hamilton, the daily visitor as Nellie's fiancé. There were jokes and pranks, fun and laughter. I begin with some extracts from the stays in Edinburgh and at Strone. I have divided my extracts from that part of the diary written during her London stay into two sections: the first those about people and herself, the second about expeditions and some of the sightseeing which most impressed her.

> Saturday, Sept. 21st 1872. Started per 10.29 train from Elgin. Saw Nelly Rich at the station. Got into nice through carriage at Forres. Took honey beside me.4 nice ladies in carriage. Slept part of the way from Forres to Perth. Took lunch with me consisting of biscuits and sherry. Lady opposite me seemed shocked and obviously thought it was O.D.V.!!! Mr. Alves appeared at Stirling and came into my carriage. Enjoy the rest of the journey exceedingly. Arrived very laIe in the forenoon at Waverley Station. Got to Salisbury Place very tired.

> Sunday, 22nd September. Went to Dr. Alexander's church in the forenoon. Stranger preached. Met Mr. Alves coming out of church. Went to call on Mr.Andrew. Went to St.John's Episcopal Church.

[Dr William Lindsay Alexander was minister at the Congregational Church He had been classical tutor at Blackburn Theological College 1827–1932 when he went to North College Street Congregational Church Edinburgh to assist the Rev. John Cleghorn. Later he was called to the Augustine College Church (1835–1877). In 1877 he became Professor of Systematic Theology in the Theological Hall of the Congregational Churches of Scotland College.]

Sunday 23rd September 1872. Left from Waverley Station – arrive in Glasgow and meet Aggie at 2.15. Walked through part of the town. Took train again to Greenock. Got steamer there "The Vivid" and arrived at Strone at 6.30. After tea went for a row with Marshall.

Tuesday, Sept. 24th, 1872. Arranged to go to Rothesay. Start in big boat at 9 a.m. to Hunter's Quay. Got the Iona there – fine steamer. Beautiful scenery, rugged hills, Arran in the distance. Arrive at Rothesay and walk to the top of Serpentine Hill – extensive view.

Wednesday, Sept. 25th 1872. Receive notes from Mr Alves. Aggie and I go to Lochgoilhead, splendid sail, very cold. Come home to dinner. Eliza, Marshall and I go for a row to the top of the Loch, which I enjoy above all. Return home and find beautiful Birthday presents of card case, and cards from Mr. Alves. Write to thank him, which I cannot do enough to repay all his kindness .

Thursday, Sept. 26th 1872. My birthday, age 21, feel getting old. Received kind present from Mrs Grieve, Aggie, and Eliza. Marshall and I go for a row in the punt. Go to tea at Mrs.Pulsford's. Wrote to Mama. "Life is real. Life is earnest" October 1st. Up at 5.45 and get ready for leaving with regret. At 7.45 per steamer to Greenock for Edinburgh. Arrive Edinburgh. Take dinner at Mrs Grieve's. Make ready tea for Mrs A.S.Grieve and Marshall who arrive at 9 o'clock. Letters from Mama and from Mr Andrew, who wishes me to take lunch with them tomorrow, Friday.

Octr 4th 1872. Go into town with Mrs Grieve, Aggie and Rachel. Come home to dinner. Pack up things for journey. Say goodbye to Salisbury View. Mr Andrew and Mr Alves come at 8.p.m. We have supper, then go to the station. Andrew Haig is there. Start for London. Read letters during my journey. Feel astonished at them and very much pleased. Arrive at 1, Eagle Place have breakfast. Think very much about the contents of said letters and wish I had their meaning from the writer's lips, rather than having read what pleased me so much, yet filled me with surprise. I make up my mind to wait patiently and all will be ordered aright.

Octr. 13th, '72. We start immediately after breakfast (Nellie,

Hamie and I) for the Foundling Hospital Chapel, where we arrive in good time. Most impressive sermon by Mr. Maurice. Pretty sight, the Foundlings, the girls on one side of the organ with their snowy caps bins and aprons, I mean Richards not bibs. The singing is beautiful, the children's voices sound so sweet and the words very distinct. All go to see the Foundlings dine – a very pretty sight, they seem so happy.

Oct. 28th 1872. Still no letter not even a newspaper. Oh! Hope deferred maketh the heart sick. "Courant" from Mama telling me that Papa has retired from the Town Council. Saturday, November 2nd 1872 Mr. Alves sent me music this morning, and with it a note by which we see he is not coming to London, at which we are much disappointed.

Nov. 12th 1872. Went to dine with Mrs. Young, Mrs John Young and John at 13, Gloucester Street, all very well. The Youngs asked me to come again whenever I liked. They hadn't a bed and were very sorry. John's wife is delightful.

Wednesday, Nov. 13th, 1872. Mrs Hulse called for me at 12o'clock and took me to Ealing. Very kind people. Had dinner and went for a walk and round by the village. Very pretty place and fine houses. Had tea. So sorry for these poor people losing so many sons and daughters and left alone, as it were, in the world.

Thursday, Nov. 14th, 1872. Mrs Young and I set off for Highgate by omnibus and trams, we arrive there in due course. Walked up Highgate Hill and passed Whitington's stone where the celebrity rested. Got to Highgate Cemetery and found the grave where Mama's little girl and her father Mr Hulse are buried.

Friday, 15th November, 1872. This is Katie's birthday and a few parties came to a small party – shining brilliantly they came to the cooking-shine. I shone too. That's not egotism. We gambled, gambolled, gobbled, finishing up with a "Here we go round". Mrs Rich's humour!!!. "Donkeys, Janet"!!! Katie's nose is better now being a "jolly nose". Mrs. Rich appears in our room being masked as a donkey, and she made Mr Rich jump out of his bath right in the air, by calling "Police, Police" through the keyhole. Had to soothe him and lead him back again. Never laughed so much in my long and useful life. Mrs. Rich says she is the pattern of (winking) morals.

Oct. 9th 1872. Nellie and I go out after dinner (grouse and champagne) We go along Regent Street to the Thames Embankment. Very beautiful passing Trafalgar Square where there is Nelson's Monument with Landseer's splendid lions. See the Strand, Somerset House, Waterloo Bridge.

Oct. 11th 1872. Kate and I go to the Crystal Palace Bazaar and Soho Bazaar. After dinner Nellie and I go for a walk through Hyde Park and come home along Oxford and Regent Streets, very fine architecture.

Oct. 12th 1872. Nellie, Katie, Mr Hamilton and I go to see the Houses of Parliament. The magnificence of which surpasses my highest expectations. Splendid Queen's Gateway and Victoria Tower with gilded top. Pass through the House of Lords, gilt throne, stained glass windows, woolsack. Beautiful lobbies with fine paintings.

(long lists of paintings and of statues of historical figures which caught her interest).

Monday, oct. 14th 1872. Kate and I leave 1, Eagle Place to go to Westminster Abbey. We enter intent on exploring its curious tombs etc. A kind of mysterious awe comes over me as I wander through the lofty aisles, gazing now on the richly stained glass windows, now upwards on the carved arches and roof, which is so grand and lofty that it seems to be surrounded by a "religious light". Here I shall merely give some of the prominent names on the tombs. ——

Friday, October 18th 1872. Dismal day. Letter from Papa. Mr.Alves is at Main, arrived on Sunday morning having walked from Forres. He went to the Reidhaven Ball with John on Monday night, and dined at Main on Thursday.

Sunday, October 20th 1872. We go to church to hear Mr. Stopford A.Brooke, Nellie's idol. Very edifying sermon.

[Mr Brooke was born in Ireland in 1832. He became well known as an author. By 1865 two of his books had been published. His first curacy was in 1859 at St Mary Abbot, Kensington. He left after four years, having made an impression for the broad views he held. From 1866 he was minister of the popular chapel of St James, York Street and had preached several times there before her Majesty Queen Victoria. In 1867 he was made Chaplain-in–Ordinary at St James's chapel and remained as such until 1889 when he was called to Bedford Chapel Bloomsbury. His book Primer of English Literature 1889) was a great success – by 1917 half a million copies had sold.]

Sunday, Octr. 26th 1872. We all go to church and Mr.Brooke preached a beautiful sermon "Dwell in Light". Building castles in the air is a great pleasure, lifting our minds for a time to things above.

Saturday, Octobr. 26th, 1872. Nellie, Mr Hamilton and I go to the Crystal Palace. The grounds are beautiful and the appearance of the Palace is light and graceful "exceeding" and very extensive, while to me the interior seems like Fairy Land. – barring the cats and Satan which I am led to believe do not exist in that ideal land. We proceeded at first to the Concert. We heard Cummings, L.Thomas, Miss Whinnery and the Crystal Palace Choir – "marvellous sweet music". Then we went to the aquarium – fishes of all kinds in large tanks, likewise Hermit Crabs, prawns, sea anemones, sponges, crabs, lobsters, eels in great variety. Particularly interested in the movements of the graceful lobsters and skates. Next to view the four hundred cats – cats young, cats old, cats hot, cats cold, cats huddled, cats cuddled, cats black, cats white, cats wild, cats tame, all very interesting to those of a feline (feeling) heart. Great number of grandees at the Palace, this being Saturday, the fashionable day. We pass through Halls Egyptian, Grecian, Roman, German, French, English. All very beautiful and interspersed with groups of trees, ferns and flowers, fountains and lakes. Splendid large organ. Fine selections from Mendelssohn played by Sangster. We reluctantly tore ourselves away and hurried home.

Tuesday, Oct. 29th 1872. Go to St Paul's Cathedral. Very much delighted with this immense stately building and enormous dome, fine windows and statues of Nelson and other great men. None of the windows are as beautiful as those at my favourite Westminster. St. Paul's is at the moment under a process of cleaning and repairing.

Sunday, Novr. 3rd 1872. Mr Hamilton, Katie and I go to service at Westminster Abbey, made more grand by the organ pealing and the sun's rays lighting up the rich windows. The text was Psalm CV11-30, "The Haven of Rest". I sincerely wish I would be at rest there.

Monday, Novr. 4th and Tuesday 5th, 1872. We go to the National Gallery on each of these days. (List of my favourite paintings). We also visit the Lowther Arcade. Evening of Tuesday we go to the theatre (Drury Lane) in the evening and see "Fun in a Fog" a very amusing farce by five of the Vokes family. Enjoyed a hearty laugh. The "The Lady of the Lake" by A.Halliday with the most lovely scenery- Loch Katrine, The Trossachs, the distant hills are very beautiful with the boat crossing the loch. Ellen appears in her boat and meets Fitz-James – they reach Ellen's Isle and enter "the enchanted Hall" The play advances keeping as close to the original as possible. The Incanto Scene was superb – three real living figures in the air. We came home quite charmed.

Many other excursions the girls took exploring London are described briefly. I am sure they must have been weary by the end of some days when they walked for miles. Covent Garden was a favourite of Tudy; she also enjoyed visits to Burlington Arcade, to the Botanical Gardens, the Geological Museum, "finest in the world", the Bethnal Green Museum, Soho Bazaar, by boat to Battersea Park, and spent a long day at the British Museum. She and Nellie greatly enjoyed the Gustave Doré Gallery in Bond Street in particular the painting "Christ Leaving the Praetorium". They went to a concert, The Monday Popular, at St James Hall: Henry Holmes, Piatti, M. M. Ri—(?) and Zorbini played a Haydn quartet, Madame Sinico sang Mozart's 'Nozze di Figaro', and 'Del Vieni non tardu', and Madame Arabella Goddard "delighted us" with Beethoven's Sonata in G minor, the C major and finally a Mendelssohn sonata. I was interested to read that Nellie and Hamie and Tudy were in the Strand and went to see the Chapel Royal, Savoy. She wrote, "it is a beautiful little chapel, walls and roof painted and finely gilded. Nellie and Hamie would like to be married there". [How interested my granny would have been to know that her grand-daughter Maryan, my sister, was married there in

1963 – for just the same reason – that she and her fiancé had been to look at the Chapel Royal and had felt the same as Nellie and Hamie did.]

Some evenings at 1 Eagle Place there was music – piano and singing. Sometimes they read in the evenings. Tudy's book of the moment was *Robin Grey*. She also read *The Times* each day, and was an admirer of Tennyson. Occasionally they played the popular game of 'Confessions'. There is one mention of a game of vingt-et-un. To Tudy it was great fun. But on Friday, 22 November this happy exciting visit came to an end. Mr Rich made some sandwiches for Tudy's lunch on the train, and he, Mrs Rich, Nellie and Katie saw her off. The route was by Carlisle and then to the Caledonian Station Edinburgh. She was looking forward to seeing Mr Alves again, had wearied of this long break, was troubled by his silence, but hope still warmed her heart. Could it be that he would be at the station to meet her, together with Eliza and Annandale? Or was this building castles in the air? (an expression Tudy sometimes used). As it happened there was nobody to meet her, so she took a cab to Blacket Place. Her cousins had mistakenly gone to the North British Station. She was at once caught up in the busy round of the Grieve households. There is no mention of Mr Alves in the diary entries for the next two weeks. Perhaps he was away on business? I wish I could see the letters she wrote to her dear Nellie in London. On 26 November she received a letter from Nellie and in it was enclosed a copy of a poem from The *Scotsman*. She had written beneath it "From my dear Nellie, Scotsman Novr. 26th 1872."

Love's Expositors

How is it that in all the earth,
All that is beautiful in birth
Or being, is part of him?
The waters seem to lisp his name.
Winds whisper and all things claim
To be my love's interpreter.

The birds all sing of him, the flowers
Must know these secret thoughts of ours —
The very air seems laden so
With music of unburdened speech
That lies for ever out of reach,
Yet follows me where e'er I go.

Singing he passed me in the wood
But yesterday unseen I stood,
And all things stood to see him pass
The wild flowers laughed beneath his tread,
I thought the very earth was glad
To have his shadow on the grass.

Birds followed him and all things bent
The way his blessed footsteps went,
And watched him to the very last.
The winds sank down and only sigh'd
And eager daisies, open-eyed,
Stared after him until he passed.

Who has not known the magic of love, the uncertainties, the helplessness when it brings pain or disillusion? Here is a selection from this last part of the diary.

> Wednesday, November 28th,. Busy sewing all day. Went to a lecture at the institute on Michael Faraday the chemist. Most interesting, as well as amusing, illustrating Michael's beautiful character, and how in the midst of his greatness he never forgot the Gracious Giver of All.

> Thursday, November 28th 1872. Wrote several long letters. In the evening went to a lecture at the church by Dr. Alexander on Rev. V from 1-12. Very interesting and instructive.

> Monday, December 2nd,. Very foggy morning, called on the Browns, and saw Janet and Bella. Invitation to tea and we go,

Aggie, Rachael and I. Charades and music. Note from Mrs. Bishop inviting me for Friday evening and I accept.

Wednesday, December 4th. Call at Salisbury View, and then at Mrs. Haig's. Aggie came for me and we took a car to Morningside. Called for Dr. Skae, then went to the Asylum. We saw old Mrs. Donaldson who is insane. Walked home. In the evening Aggie, Jane and I went to the Institute to hear a lecture. Annan and Harold were with us. I enjoyed the lecture muchly. Subject "The Light of Life, a critique on Men of Science of the Present Day". The lecturer, Dr. Smith of Glasgow, took up Carlyle, R.W. Emerson and Matthew Arnold. The former regards mankind as a number of shams and his cure would be to raise "men sincere of heart and loyal in thought" and thus let the world be guided. The seoond considers men to be mainly copyists in their development. Such is the American's "Light of Life". The third regarded men as afflicted with sheer stupidity and rather enamoured of it!! His idea was to perfect the intellect of a few, a "peculiar people" – some children of light among the prevailing Philistinism. Self-honesty-Carlyle Self-development – Emerson, Self-culture– Arnold. Three cynical thinkers. Went at seven 'clock to Mrs.Bishop's for tea. Mrs Burton and her two daughters there, Mr. Thomson, "John", and Mr Alves. The principal amusements were squeezing the ladies (fine specimens of Miss Mowat's "Seminary for Young Ladies") to show off their musical powers, but supposing the poor victims to have been in a singing class all day, one could not expect much voice to be left. How I pitied them – fellow feeling! I thought it best to sing without being subjected to the pressing system. My song was short and sweet in order to give Mr. Alves an early opportunity to show off his talents, which he was particularly anxious to do!!! Dancing had now begun with great gusto, in the shape of "Nine pins". We all pinned and spinned till we were tired – then supper to which I was led by "John". I sung again in a hurry in order to let the "Bailiff's Daughter" hasten to London Town and "Promised to be my bride" – too good to be true. Mr. Alves and Mr. Thomson conveyed me home. Mr A. anxious that I should go to the theatre, and declared he would write and ask Mama! Went to bed tired and thoughtful. Mrs. Grieve said she would ask Mr Alves on Friday 13th.

Sunday, December 8th. Went to church, Mr Alexander preached. Bella and I walked home and met Mr. Alves who accompanied us. In the afternoon Dr A. again. I found my thoughts wandering most uncomfortably. He said "Without religion where would we be? Without it Luther would have died unknown. What pleasure we would lose, all the works of God speak of it and appeal to our inmost thoughts. These are the least of the evils". Aggie sends invitations to Andro and Gab. Haig and Mr. Alves for the Asylum Ball.

Wednesday, December 11th.. Note from Mr Alves asking my valuable counsel as to whether he should "swallow" or not on Friday evening. He is not mad enough to go to the Asylum. Mrs Grieve and two daughters, Miss Smith and Andrew Haig join us, and we all set off. Aggie, Rachel and I go on the top of the tram – great fun. Arrive at Asylum and the ball begins with a march. Several songs varied the amusement. The behaviour of some of the lunatics is most eccentric. We walked home in the same manner.

Friday, December 13th. Party in the evening. Mr Alves took my advice "unadorned". Splendid waltz with Andro Haig. Jane Grieve could not come on account of being ill. Her Mama was also detained by the same. The ghost appeared. Mr Alves had a "splitting headache" because he could not get the chance of waltzing with Miss Lodge, so the disappointment lodged in his head. Pufello!

Saturday, Dec. 14th 1872. Packed up to got to Salisbury Place. Sorry to leave Blacket Place.

Sunday, Decr.15th. We all go to church. Dr. Alexander Zech.1-18. We go back in the afternoon. Dr A. sermonised from Luke XV and 7th verse. Very common mistake that angels ONLY rejoice over the repentant sinner. Beautiful anthem at dismissal. Had dreadful toothache all the evening.

Monday, December 16th 1872. Busy making jackets for the little children at the Infirmary.

The entries, which follow, describe paying calls, visiting, completing the jackets, music at home, Dr Alexander at church "sermonising", and a shopping event when Tudy bought "an eider down skirt" and "swell shoes". She also received a letter from Mama "with orders to buy bonnets and jackets etc". There is a description of a concert in the Music Hall where "Madame Neruda performed splendidly on the violin", and of an outing to hear Basil Rivers, "a very good ventriloquist. A party of twelve went, headed by Mrs. R. Grieve."

Little was made of Christmas Day, except for a list of small presents she received. At her request papa wrote giving her permission to stay on for an extra week so that she might attend a party Mr Andrew was giving. There were frequent letters from papa and from mama (separately) and Aunt Margaret. There are also other notes to say she had bad toothache, but no mention of a visit to the dentist. She became more reserved about Mr Alves. In her philosophy, either with regard to painful love or toothache, what could not be cured must be endured, and she notes once that she must be patient "and God will set all aright".

The diary entries end:

> Thursday, December 27th 1872. Preparing for evening party. Call on Miss Balmain, she is delighted to see me. Party in the evening: Mrs. Murray, Miss Murray, 4 Brown, 2 Haigs, 8 Grieves, 1 Russell, Mr.Kennedy (Joe), Mr. Gray, Mr. and Mrs. Glegg etc.Dancing and charades, fun and laughter, applause – music and singing. Mrs Bishop has invited me to dinner on Saturday. Anxious I should go to Mr. Andrew's. Ask Papa. Receive a telegram saying "accept invitation".

> Monday, December 30th 1872. Delightful party at Mr Andrew's.

> Thursday January 2nd 1873. Went along to call on Mr. Andrew. Saw Dean Ramsay's funeral. Procession. Walked on to Mr. Andrew's, Mr. Alves there. Stayed a short time. He said he would be at the station on Monday morning to see me off.

The diary ends with six blank pages, and with it, I fear, her friendship with Mr Alves.

CHART E: ABBREVIATED CHART OF THE EDINBURGH GRIEVES

The full tree of the Edinburgh Grieves has been well researched, and there are descendants in Canada and New Zealand. The early generations were prominent members of the Royal Physical Society of Edinburgh. Two grandsons of David Grieve, Jedderfield and Margaret White became wine merchants in Edinburgh.

Robert Grieve of Noblehall 1776-1853 m.1803 Agnes Symington 1783-1846 ch.

1. **Robert Symington Grieve 1816-1865 m.1841 Jane Sommerville 1817-1903 ch.**
   (1) Henry David Grieve b.1847 (2) Agnes Grieve b.1848 (3) James Grieve b.1852 (4) Annandale Grieve b.1855 (5) Edith Grieve b.1859 (6) Francis Grieve b.1860
   (This family was at 7 Blacket Place and then Salisbury View)
2. **William Grieve 1822-1862 m.1848 Eliza Sommerville 1822-1901** (a sister of the above Jane; they were daughters of William Sommerville of the Polton Mills, Penicuik and his wife Jane Ferguson) **ch:**

(1) **Symington Grieve 1849-1932** (see below) (2) Jane Grieve b.1850 (3) Eliza Grieve b.1852 (4) Isabella (Bella) Grieve 1853-1938 (5) Sommerville Grieve 1855-1932 (6) Harold Grieve b.17.3.1856 (7) Amelia (Amy) Grieve b.1858 (8) Herbert Grieve b.1861 (9) William Grieve b.1863
(This family lived at 9 Blacket Place)

The above (1) Symington Grieve 1849-1932 m.19.10.1882 Christian Smith Anderson 1854-1935

Their daughter Marjorie Grieve 1894-1963 m.1924 Russell Thin 1891-1969. A daughter of this marriage, Jean Thin m. Robert

Bartholomew. So the two well-known Edinburgh publishers were united. Their daughter Jane and her husband, Professor Alan Torrance, St Mary's College, St Andrews, and their sons, Andrew b.1984, Peter b.1986, Robert b.1988 and David b.1991, live near St Andrews.

CHAPTER 8

A TIME OF CHANGE

At first it was good to be home again with the family, but before long Tudy found it hard to come to terms with the loss of hope. She copied the following into a notebook headed "Scraps from books I have read, 1873":

> In the awful mystery of human life, it is a consolation sometimes to believe that mistakes, perhaps even our sins, are not irretrievable, are permitted to be instruments of our education for immortality. God teaches us sometimes by our very errors, leading us through them onto light. However difficult it may be we must not be disheartened. We must leave the past where it is, and go on to the future; do what we have to do, and suffer all we have to suffer. We must direct things as they are without perplexing ourselves about what they might have been.
>
> From Christian's Mistake by Miss Mulock.

There is more, but this extract seems to indicate her grief, and her goodness of purpose. For Tudy and her father religion was central to their lives. However, their views were moderate. For some time Alex had advocated a change in the form of service at St Giles. One Sunday before the morning service at church Alex hinted that there might be a welcome announcement. At the end of the service Mr Mackie asked if the congregation would remain seated. He addressed then in solemn tones.

> After discussion, I have to tell you that the Kirk Session have come to a decision as regards a subject frequently under discussion, that of posture in public worship. The congregation is requested – and I stress only requested – to stand during praise

and to kneel during prayer; also that after service the worshippers should resume their seats for a short space and ask a blessing on the services before leaving. I must remind you that sitting at praise and standing at prayer were not practised in the Scotch church until introduced by English Puritans in the seventeenth century – and that without any authority. There is no law regulating posture in worship and I can quote the Scriptures to show that kneeling was practised in Old Testament times, and only the Pharisees stood.

All went smoothly. The next change was the introduction of the harmonium. It was first played by Herr Noa during the Sunday school service on August 25 1874. It was to be a great source of satisfaction to the Sunday school but proved inadequate in the church. Not having sufficient power it was scarcely heard in the volume of voices raised during praise. In the fullness of time St Giles had its organ. Not everyone approved of the instrument. The name of the originator of a well-known phrase denigrating the instrument may be forgotten, but the words are not – "It's no' but a kist o' whistles". Nevertheless, many found joy in the music of the church.

Alex heard that a pleasant house in Queen Street in Elgin was to be sold. It seemed to him that it was time that the family made a move from Main. He had accepted a post as legal adviser at the Royal Bank of Scotland. One of the clauses in the agreement was that the bank would employ any of his sons who wished to work there. Tom and Alick worked at this bank, in Alick's case for all the years until his retirement. The journeys to and from Elgin made by the various members of the family were numerous; to stay in Elgin would simplify this. So Mary and Alex went to see the house – 14 Queen Street – a spacious house with a good garden. He broke the news to the children with some trepidation. Tudy at once saw the advantages – that they would all be near the grandmamas was her first thought. The boys were anxious to know whether their horses would be kept on. Alick was as usual compliant, but Tom, who loved the farm, declared that he would certainly be farming himself before long and this came about.

The remainder of the lease of Main was sold to the Hon. Captain Chetwynd. There were so many happy memories of the days at Main, but the family soon settled down in Elgin. Alex found it handy to get to his many meetings, and all the family joined in the busy social and eventful round.

There was an unusual entertainment at the Assembly Rooms, presented by the Gompertz Company. It consisted of a dioramic view of a tour through the Continent. This included views of the Franco-Prussian battlefields. Another event that appealed to Tudy and her parents was 'Illustrations of the Pilgrim's Progress' with Christian's journey "gorgeously portrayed in limelight". The choir gave fine renderings to accompany the pictures. 'Especially moving were the subdued strains of the hymn 'Courage Brother, do not stumble', and later, as Christian passed over the chilly river of death, the swelling notes of 'Jerusalem my glorious Home'. Another treat, long remembered, was a harp recital by Aptomnas, (the Paganini of the Harp).

During the next years there were three deaths. Grandmama Russell passed away at her home on 15 February 1874; she was 85 years old. Grandmama Merson departed this life on 5 November 1876. My granny told me that both her grannies, who had always been close to her heart, had borne their troubles with faith and fortitude. But sometimes Grandmama Russell when reminiscing would suddenly be reminded of past years, would struggle to hold back tears, and shaking her head would say, "Oh my bonnie laddies".

The death of Margaret Russell on 5 July 1877 must have been a hard blow to Tudy and Alex. Margaret had been the centre of the Russell and the Merson families since Alex lost his young wife Keturah. Margaret was kind, sympathetic, lively and cheerful. Over the long years she kept in touch with the various families, paying regular visits to the Conquergoods in Leith, to the Grieves in Edinburgh and to the Russells in Peebles.

Henry Cameron was 21 in 1877 and inherited some money from his father's estate. He made the decision to emigrate to New Zealand.

He shipped to Melbourne on the *Great Britain*, and then trans-shipped to Otago. Here he got work as a cadet on first Galloway station and then on Ben Lomond station. With this experience behind him he started to farm on a property then known as Canada Farm near Milburn. His letters home were cheerful, and must have had an unsettling effect on Johnnie and on Tom. Johnnie had complied with his father's wishes and was training with a legal firm. His heart was not in it and there was sometimes friction between him and his father. I know that Tudy had a great affection for her handsome brother and once said, "Poor Johnnie, he never had a chance".

In the winter of 1776 Alex was ill. Dr Grigor diagnosed his sudden attack of severe chest pains as angina pectoris, and Alex had to comply and spend a few weeks in bed and then, when up, was advised to 'take it easy'. This was hard for him and quite alien to his disposition. How thankful he was to resume work and the duties of his various offices. Before very long he had a new mission. He heard that property known as Panns was up for sale. It was a small compact estate with a good sound farmhouse. But for Alex its situation was what pleased him. It lay on the banks of the Lossie to the east of Elgin. He was fascinated when he found it had originally belonged to the monks of Pluscarden and its original name was Chanonry. Although born and brought up in Elgin, Alex had a great love for the farming countryside. He persuaded Mary that this would be the ideal home for them in the future when he retired. He cherished the idea that his son Johnnie would in time succeed him at Chanonry. So he negotiated and bought it.

Alex was delighted to be back at work. Since he had become a joint agent for the Royal Bank, business had increased in that department to an extent that the Directors decided to erect larger premises, and the handsome building on the north side of the Plainstones was built. The move was made towards the end of October 1877 and Alex was delighted with the premises. Once again he was happily engaged with his church duties, with the meetings at the Lodge, with drawing up a new will. He had supervised the transference of the Water Company to the Elgin Corporation and now, as chairman of the Gas Company, was involved in stressful negotiations regarding the transfer of that company to Elgin Corporation. He had been chairman of the Parochial Board for almost fifteen years and was deeply interested in this work.

Each year Alex prepared the accounts for the annual meeting of the Guildry. His father had been proud when Alex as a young man had become a member and taken office. Now Johnnie was a member, but Alex wondered what part the boy would take in future years, for he had recently expressed a wish to go to India and become a tea planter. Alex gave him little encouragement but eventually came round. Arrangements were finalised. Johnnie sailed for Calcutta in the third week in December. It was a sad time for them all but especially for Tudy. Mama had been so brave when Henry left home, and she tried her best to be cheerful.

Just after New Year 1878 Alex was kept on bed for a few days with an attack of influenza, but soon declared he was feeling fit. On 12 January Dr Grigor called to see him, and advised him not to go to the service on the next day but to stay indoors and rest. So on that Sabbath day the family had dinner together and passed the day quietly. Bedtime came and all seemed well. In the early hours Alex was woken by severe pains in the chest. The doctors were summoned, but before they could reach him Alex had died. Tudy's first thoughts were that her brother Johnnie was so far away – that he would not get news of his father's death until he reached Calcutta, that he was not with her, was not there to help at this awful time. Nor was Aunt Margaret.

The account of Mr Russell's death and of his life in Elgin filled an entire page of small type in the *Moray Weekly News*. Two extracts are as follows:

> When it became known throughout the town that Mr Russell had passed away, sympathy, universal and deep, was expressed, for it is not too much to say that there remains not in Elgin one who had so extensive a circle of sincerely attached friends. It will be

long before the community finds another to take such a lively interest in all pertaining to their weal. Sympathy is all the citizens can give to the family of the deceased. That sympathy they freely bestow, mourning his loss as a warm-hearted friend, valued counsellor and faithful guide.

[There follows a description of his public life and his many offices.]

Mr Russell was 62 years of age when he died. It cannot be said to have been a long life measured by years, yet it is a long life measured by good deeds. Seldom has a gentleman left as many marks on institutions as did Mr Russell. His life was one eminently devoted to the good of his fellowmen. Genial in temperament, courteous by manner, and ever willing to give advice, he was consulted by almost every class of the community. To industrious and well-doing young men he was ever ready to lend a helping hand. In Mr Russell the city of Elgin has lost its most useful citizen, the Parish Church a warm supporter and consistent ornament and society in general a most estimable member.

The description of the funeral, which took place on 18 January, is as follows:

At the request of the Town Council it was a public one. A large number of Citizens and Gentlemen from adjoining districts availed themselves of the opportunity of paying a last tribute to their departed friend. The cortége started from the residence of the deceased in Queen Street at one o'clock. It was headed by the elders of the Established Church after whom walked the Magistrates and Town Councillors in a body, Provost Culbard immediately preceding the hearse. Then came several carriages and the general company.' [There follows a long list of selected names and the route taken through the streets of Elgin to the New Cemetery].

All along the route spectators were numerous, windows etc being largely used as places of vantage. The various bells of the town meanwhile tolled slowly. All businesses being for the nonce entirely suspended in the city, the effect was solemn and imposing. The day was fine and bright. Messrs Mackie and Stewart officiated. The chief mourners were Alexander and Thomas, sons of the late Mr Russell.

Tudy copied out in her notebook the following extract from the Banffshire Journal of January 22 1878.

The Rev Mr. McNaughton at the close of his sermon, delivered on Sabbath afternoon in the Elgin Parish Church, with regard to the death of Ex-Provost Russell, made the following graceful and touching reference to the character of the deceased. Mr McNaughton had been speaking from the text 'There is a friend that sticketh closer than a brother'. He said, "We have been speaking of friendship and friends. Since last Lord's Day we met for worship in this house of prayer, you have lost a friend; the church has lost a friend, the city has lost a friend - one of the best friends the city or the Church has ever had or for ever will have. It is quite unnecessary for me to dwell on the public career or private character of the Late Mr Russell, especially after what has been so fully and appreciatively said in the public prints, and by God's servant in this house this morning. Indeed Mr Russell's life and work have been so fully treated that there is almost nothing left for me to say. But I cannot withhold my humble tribute of admiration for him as a man and as a Christian. I never knew a better man – one in whom the qualities of head and heart were so finely blended. To know him was to love him. You required to be in his company but for a few minutes to discern that you were in the presence of no ordinary man. Many and many a family in this place and far around have been befriended by Mr Russell in his own quiet, unselfish, unassuming way. He was a pattern in many ways – in church attendance, for instance, he set an example to the whole community ...

This day fortnight past he worshipped on this house three times. It so chanced that two of the services fell to my lot to conduct – afternoon and evening. He failed not to be in his seat. And looking back it seems to me almost prophetic that the subjects of my remarks were what they were. For the afternoon my text was 'There is but a step between me and Death'. In the evening, my subject was 'Tomorrow! Boast not thyself of tomorrow, for thou knowest not what a day may bring forth.' May each of us strive to imitate him in his sound, his sincere piety, in his usefulness, in his industry, in his amiability of disposition, in the honourableness of his life, in the beauty and symmetry of his entire nature.

Bravely, with pride and pain, Tudy copied this out, and resolved to strive to live up to the example her father had set, and foremost to do all she could to be a comfort to Mama. The reading of the will had, of course, taken place after the funeral. These were the terms. Five eminent citizens were named as executors together with his wife and his sons John and Alick. In the first clause he dealt with the legacy to his daughter Keturah, leaving her the sum of £3000 to be carefully invested in Heritable Security or good railway stock, the interest to be paid to her quarterly. He tied it up so that in the event of her marriage it could not be used to pay off any debts her husband might incur. It continued as follows:

> And secondly to my eldest son John Patrick Merson a like sum of £3,000 in full of all the claims he might have on my estate whether as heir-at-law or in any other capacity declaring he shall have no right to any part or portion of the heritable property belonging to me. I have deemed it better to give him his portion of the money to enable him should he feel so inclined to enter into a commercial business to be approved of by my trustees.
>
> And 3rd I leave to my second son Alexander Russell the lands of Chanonry (formerly called Panns) along with any heritable property in Elgin and the whole residue of my estate under the burden of two thousand pounds to be paid to my third son Thomas Russell. I desire that the said lands of Chanonry shall be continued in the family and I am sure my wife will do all that is within her power to carry my wishes into effect.
>
> And 4th I also ordain that the said lands of Chanonry shall be burdened with the annual payment of my wife's annuity of £280 sterling.
>
> And 5th to Henry Cameron, presently in New Zealand, I leave £10 to buy a ring, in token of my love and affection for one who was brought up under my roof and was a most affectionate and dutiful member of my family.

It was deemed by all to be a fair and just will, as one would expect from such a man as Alexander Russell.

CHAPTER 9

MR AND MRS WILLIAM ADAM

Mary Russell was faced with a problem. Much as she wanted to carry out the wish of her dear husband, she did not see how she could manage to leave Queen Street and take the family to Chanonry. She discussed it with Tudy, who understood, and then she took the matter to the trustees. After some consideration they agreed that it was best in the circumstances to postpone any move. And so the diminished family continued to live at Queen Street. A fine mural monument was erected over Alexander Russell's grave, and above the inscription the arms of the Bedford Russells with their motto CHE SARA SARA. This is puzzling; for those who are interested in genealogy I have made some comments in Chart A p26.

In the summer of 1880 Tudy went to Cologne (which she wrote in a notebook as Cöln) and spent some happy months there improving her spoken German and having art lessons. More than that I do not know, but she refers to it in a notebook written ten years later. She was talented in painting flower pictures, and at some time she ordered china plates from a factory, painted flowers on them and sent them back to be glazed.

The next family event concerned Tom Russell. He had not been happy working in the bank, so went as a farm cadet to Mr George Todd of Ardivit; this proved to be a useful experience when he decided to emigrate to New Zealand. On 14 September 1881, aged eighteen, he sailed from London on the S.S. *Hurunai* as one of the 7 saloon and 31 second class and steerage passengers. The ship docked at Port of Otago on 26 December 1881 (100 days at sea!) where he was met by his half-brother Henry Cameron. For four years the two of them farmed in partnership on Canada Farm, Inch Clutha. Then, on his own, Tom leased, and later bought, Lime Kiln Farm at Milburn. In October 1899 he married Catherine Jane Elizabeth Fleming. She was the daughter of Alexander Fleming and Margaret Anderson, Scots from Drumturk, Alyth, Perthshire who had emigrated to New Zealand.

How much had Tom Russell been influenced by his father Alex? His upbringing at Main surely shaped his inclinations towards farming. He was a good farmer; he farmed Milburn successfully for 52 years, and sold it a very satisfactory price. When my mother's sister, Ann Adam, went out to New Zealand (c.1912?) she stayed at Milburn and enjoyed good riding, and wrote home saying that Tom was a fine horseman. At many provincial shows he won prizes for his Clydesdale light carriage horses, for his Border Leicester sheep, and his shorthorn and Jersey cattle. He also won a large marble timepiece, the Peter McGill prize successes with his Pearl Velvet wheat in three consecutive years. Our New Zealand Russell clan was founded by Tom and his wife Catherine. Their first son, Hulse Alexander, died at the age of 15 months. Their second son Albert Eden was born 1 October 1892. Mary Jane Hulse was born 12 September 1895; Fleming Alexander in 1898; Catherine Margaret 21 July 1902, and Veda Tomina 28 August 1907. Eden wrote of his parents:

> My father and mother both took an active interest in all matters concerning the welfare of the Milburn and adjoining communities, especially church and school. Dad was a member and Chairman of the school committee for a number of years. Both took an interest and active part in the establishment and erection of the Milburn Presbyterian Church of which he was made one of the first elders. Dad also interested himself in farming and local affairs. He was for a time President of the Tokomariso Farmers' Agricultural and Pastoral Society and the Farmers Union. He was a member of and Chairman of the Bruce County Council, and from 1908–1922 of the South Otago Hospital Board. Throughout her 45 years of married life at Lime Kiln Farm Mother was widely known for her kindness and hospitality. She took a great interest in church and other local

affairs. After Mother's death on October 10th 1869 Dad carried on the farm until all members of the family were established in other interests. On December 31st 1941 Dad was married for a second time, to Mary Anderson, a distant relative of my mother's. On April 20, 1943 the farm was sold and they went to live at Oamaru. Dad died on March 27th, 1855 in his 92nd year.

Eden was to have a fine career. He attended Otago University and Knox College. He fought in the 1914-18 War in the NZMC in Egypt and in France. When he returned he was drawn to journalism (as his grandfather Alex had been) and joined the staff of the *Clutha Leader*, Balclutha. He became editor and manager and was able to purchase ownership, subsequently buying a partnership in a rival paper, and formed the South Otago Newspapers Ltd, which later became a public company. On 28 March 1923 Eden was married to Eileen Blanche McElrea BSc. She was the second daughter of William McElrea, headmaster of the Normal School, Dunedin, and his wife Emily McCoy, who came from a distinguished academic family.

We will now rush backward through the years to Elgin in the 1880s, and to a happy event. Late in 1881 the engagement was announced between Keturah Elizabeth Russell and William Gordon Adam. William was the fourth of nine children of William Adam (1804–1892) and his wife Ann Hardy MacKessack of Crossley, Pluscarden. The ancestor of this Adam farming family is Alexander Adam of Whythwrath (1626–1668). He is buried in Birnie Kirkyard; the grave is marked by a flat stone, which can only be seen by removing the turf! It is inscribed HERE LYES ANE HONEST MAN ALEXANDER ADAM.

My cousin Duncan Adam once took me to a spot on the Elgin Golf Course and pointed up to the hills. He told me that the soil of the land at the hill farm of Barden had been poor, but now it stands out as a green patch. This was because William Adam had patiently, every day for two years, brought two cartloads of lime and spread it to improve the land. Eventually with his savings he was able to take the

Keturah Russell

William Adam

lowland farm of Kinnedar. On the day of the removal a pig escaped; it was a hot day and they could not get it to leave its bathing place in a burn. Later they were obliged to go back and collect it - just one extra chore on a busy day!

When William Adam met Keturah Russell he was living at Burghead where he had settled as a young man. There he had established the first chemical fertiliser factory in Scotland. He was a clever man, hard working, respected and well liked, and an eminent citizen of Burghead. In 1862 a branch line of the Highland Railway was laid; it went by Burghead to Hopetoun, thus making Burghead a suitable place for business, which comprised a ship-building yard, a tar distillery and a cooperage. Young William Adam established what was to be the largest chemical fertiliser plant in Scotland. The business first ran on carbide lamps until electricity came. It is not long since the line of low buildings was taken down.

William Adam was a good-looking man with fair hair and blue eyes. He was clever, hard-working, well liked and public-spirited. For many years he was a councillor, a Bailie, and then Provost of Elgin. His marriage with Keturah took place at 14 Queen Street on 19 July 1882, and was conducted by the Rev. Robert McPherson. After the ceremony and family reception Mr and Mrs William Adam left in a carriage for the railway station to go by train to Burghead, but met with an accident. A horse, which was pulling a hearse, took fright and bolted. Before it could be pulled up, the vehicles collided. Nobody was hurt. Mr. Adam declared firmly that "it was certainly a bit of bad luck but must not be said by anyone to be an ill omen". He commended his bride on her exemplary calmness and her courage. The events at Burghead were described in *The Courant*:

> This thriving seaport wore a very gay and festive appearance. The employees early decorated all the prominent parts of the Chemical Works with a fine display of bunting, and the striking appearance of the railway station reflected great credit to the officials there, the flags having been arranged in a very tasteful

manner. The whole of the vessels in the harbour, the coastguard station, and many private flagstaffs joined to make what was an imposing sight, and our quiet town has seldom looked so gay or shown to such advantage. In honour of the happy event the employees were treated to a dinner at Mr. Adam's house. Mr. Morrison took the chair, and after the tables had been cleared many loyal and patriotic toasts were given. Mr. Ross in a felicitous speech remarked on the very cordial friendship existing between Mr Adam and his employees.

'Mr. and Mrs. Adam' spent the next two or three days in their home, a neat stone-built house, appropriately entitled 'Edenville'. The honeymoon was in North America, one objective being to visit the Niagara Falls. About fifty years later my Granny Keturah was staying with my parents in County Durham. We took a picnic to Cotherstone near Barnard Castle, and went to see High Force. Granny was delighted and very excited by the cascade. "But mother," said my mother, "you have seen the Niagara Falls – surely this is nothing in comparison?" Granny said with great dignity, "Oh yes it is, it is far more impressive."

My Granny and Grandpa Adam lived at Burghead for about six years. It must have become increasingly small for their needs as each year another baby was born. My mother, Mary Gordon Adam, was the eldest and was born on 5 April 1884. She had dark brown hair and green eyes. Her siblings were all fair and blue-eyed; my mother told me there was a dark-haired child in each generation of the Russells. Her sister Ann was born in 1885, William Gordon in 1886 and Charles Merson in 1887. Edenville must have become increasingly small for their needs, and in 1878 William Adam bought Darliston, a very pleasant and much more commodious house, in the south-west of Elgin. The train ran past the bottom of the Darliston garden, and each morning stopped to pick up Mr Adam to take him to his work at Burghead. His working day was long but he was a man who never spared himself. It was a very happy family. My mother often told me of the pranks the older children played; one was to hide high up in the trees near the gate and drop

Johnnie Russell before leaving for India, 1872

chestnuts on anyone who came past below. Later there were two more babies, bringing the total to six: William Alfred (known as Wilfred), born in November 1892, and Alexander Russell (Russell) in July 1895. A very welcome visitor came to stay with them in 1886, Tudy's brother Johnnie, home on leave from India. He brought all sorts of delicacies and presents. He was delighted with his little niece Mary and gave her a small knife, fork and spoon.

My Granny Tudy must have had good servants (including a nanny) after they moved to Elgin, and she had a holiday after having the first four children. She was accompanied by her Aunt Mina (Mrs Sims) and her Elgin friend, Nellie Cruikshanks. Aunt Mina (Mrs Sim) had lost her husband and subsequently had opened a School for Young Ladies at South Bank. She took after her father, had his gift for teaching and shared his interest in old books in mathematics and in astronomy. She was also a very good gardener and after her retirement, when she moved to Gowan Brae, she worked assiduously at her needlework. Her school was a great success. My granny recalled that when the pupils were taken to concerts in the Town Hall, they wore opera cloaks and proceeded in a dignified crocodile. Headed by Mrs Sim, who wore a widow's cap, they took their places in the front row of the Hall. Among them remembered names were 'Josie Shearer, Tiny Cruikshank, Katie Clark, Violet Benton and several Mortimers.'

Tudy gives a full account of the holiday in a notebook, which I have. Below are some extracts from it, with the place names as she spelt them.

Jottings of a Continental Tour Undertaken by three unprotected Females July 1880.

We - that is myself, a nondescript individual, my auntie and a young lady friend, having taken an affectionate farewell to our hearths and homes and taken our seats in a railway compartment, glide out of Elgin station en route for the first stage of our journey to Edinburgh. We have chosen the new line over the Forth Bridge. We pass through beautiful Highland scenery to Perth, where we run to get a cup of tea. We continue by Kinross, Dunfermline, by Loch Leven and then see Arthur's Seat in the distance. Now we see the wonderful structure, the Forth Bridge - feel awe-inspired. There is no vibration, no feeling different from an ordinary journey. We reach Edinburgh in six hours. The Mascotte, our steamer from Leith Docks, was delayed and we did not sail until Tuesday.

We steam out of Leith. On deck we are cosy, wrapped up in our shawls, caps, veils and a fur rug for Mrs Sim to put over her knees. We enjoy our books and our knitting. By and by a big tea-bell rings and we meet Captain Milne. A hearty high tea and off we are to our deck seats. We pass Duntallan Castle, The Bass Rock and the Fifeshire coast. The ship rolls terribly but the Captain is very reassuring about the rolling of the ship and the state of the briny ocean. Nellie has to go below, but we still stick to the deck until 11 p.m., being occupied with star gazing and watching the different kinds of beacons. Aunt Mina is a splendid sailor and a brick. We pass the Farne Islands and St Abbs head.

Next day we are on the River Tees. On our right is Stockton-on-Tees, a large town of great iron foundries and immense steel works, There are mountains of shale and rubbish, much of it in a boiling state and being cooled with water. Cargo is put on our ship – pig iron, the small bars being put in the hold by large steam cranes, and a quantity of ammonia in bags and other chemicals.

Next day. As we are to be detained in Middlesbro' for a whole day we determine to start on an exploring excursion. First we write home to our anxious friends and families. Then we start at 11 a.m. We have a half hour walk to reach the town. We pass immense steel works – a gigantic construction. Every here and there are small engines and wagons for conveying iron. Over the river a ship is being loaded with salt put through a shaft from an elevated platform on which the engine and wagons run. We learned later that the salt is made from the brine which is pumped up from the river. We found our way to the post office, saw a handsome new Town Hall and County buildings, also the High School. We took a car to Albert Park, a gift to the town from Mr Vaughan a great iron-master. The cost was about £40,000. At the gate is an enormous tree showing what forests must have been in this neighbourhood. We walked by the flower plots, and a fountain in a lake. There were several islets with willows which droop over the water. Then we had to hurry back to the ship for dinner. Up on deck we found a different scene. The Captain and pilot were on the bridge. There were steamers of every size from tiny steam paddle tugs to the large steel steamers. Went on deck for a little while and I read Three Men in a Boat. After tea Captain Milne said the ship was to move down the river a small distance to take in more iron. We are to have 9000 tons of pig iron. The freight is 5/- per ton while Ammonia (Sulphate) is 7/6 per ton. The cargo also consists of manufactured goods such as boots; for this the freight is £2 per ton. I see numerous bales of pack-sheet. The Captain tells me that the iron he takes to Antwerp is made into things such as girdles and he often brings home to Leith a cargo of such things. The furnaces begin to smelt the iron at about 9 p.m. so we sallied forth under Captain Milne's care to see this operation and it was wonderful. Under the huge cylinder burned an immense forge, out from which poured the living fire into a large trough prepared before with wet sand. The large trough lay perpendicularly while in horizontal lines with small ones, thus: [a diagram]. A man is ready with a spade and when the molten iron has got to the end of the large trough, he opens the end small one, and so on up the line till the whole is a red beautiful living mass . The lurid place was wonderful, and all around were furnaces illuminating the sky. The men employed were mostly Irishmen and get high wages. These furnaces never go out – the cost of lighting one is about £2000.

Captain Milne told us we are to begin loading the rest of the pig-iron at 4.a.m. We are to sail at 8 a.m. and do not expect to reach Antwerp until Friday forenoon.

Thursday, July 10th. This morning we were awoken beween the hours of four and five by the noise of tons of iron rolling into the hull. No very pleasant awakening, but we were "forewarned and therefore fore-armed". At a few minutes after nine the Mascotte began slowly to move out of her moorings. We gradually lost sight of these towering erections at the mouth of the Tees. The appearance in the distance of the steam from the iron-works lent a bright silvery tint in the sky which, contrasting with the black smoke above, was striking and brought out the big towers very distinctly so that they seemed like old ruined castles.

We are passing the Yorkshire coast and presently Whitby comes into view. The castle is on the heights near the sea. Then Scarbro' - but we are too far out to see its beauties. Then we lose sight of the coast. Then the ship rolled terribly. Nellie was not well and had to retire and lie down. It was hard to keep to our seats, but then the Captain came and invited us onto the bridge. Here it was really nice, and the sun shone on us. We repaired to the bridge again after dinner and had a delightful afternoon.

On arrival at Antwerp we decided to proceed to Gand [Ghent]. We had a little fracas with the cabby who, instead of taking us to a near station in order to get a higher fare, drove us all over Antwerp, took us to a far station and charged far too much. We insisted we would not pay, and the cabby brought a policeman who suggested the cabby got only 2 centimes more, and this settled the difficulty. Took train to Gand and arrived, got a commissionaire and proceeded to Madame Mcleod's who welcomed us so heartily. Presently Dr. McLeod arrived, a dear lttle man, a clever and cultured man, they are a happy and devoted couple. We stayed at a hotel and we had three days here to see the sights – the fine Botanical Gardens,, Van Houttes, St Nicholas Church, the Cathedral.

We happened to be in Gand during the fete - some sort of annual parochial holiday and festival. Great illuminations, dancing, bands playing. All the town was in gala attire, bunting and fireworks in the Marche' an Grains, and the illuminations in the Place D'Armes where our Hotel de la Poste was. Our windows looked over the vast multitudes moving in the crowds below.

Thursday, 15th July. We leave Gand for Antwerp and our kind friend Mrs Proctor meets us and takes up to a nice hotel. We visit the Cathedral but cannot see the fine pictures. The Musee is closed. See several of Rubens in St Andrews [details of several]. We are taken for a lovely drive in the Boulevards, fine handsome houses. We have a wander thro' the gardens and the zoo. Go to a panorama of the Battle of Worms . Then dinner and to a lovely circus. Enjoyed all so much. Our friends the kindest. Got to our hotel at 12 very happy and tired.

Friday, 16th July. We travel to Bruxelle. Visited the Cathedral, very fine and plain. To the Hotel de Ville, Gothic, lovely carving. Mrs. Sim and Madame McLeod went to the top of the tower. We saw lace-making and a Gallery of pictures in the Museum. But the sight of sights was the Palais de Justice, a noble Grecian structure of enormous proportions. We take a cab and drive through the Boulevards to a Restaurant and have dinner. Then we wander about looking at shops and search for a bodice for Mrs Sim who is getting stout with all the "brchs"! [sic]

Thursday, 17th July. We started for Paris and had rather a tiresome journey, the heat being great. Country pretty, green and undulating. A thunderstorm came on in the afternoon which cooled the air. Our bags were examined by three "Douane" officers, on the boundary between Belgium and France, and horrid looking men they were, reminding one of the Inquisition men that we have read of. As we approached Paris we passed by the pretty town of Chantilly.

We arrive in the great city. Again the bags are examined, and then we get a taxi and drive off to No. 7 Avenue de Trocadero, as the cabby said. Our route is beautiful, through the Place de la Concorde with its fountains and groups of statuary all round the gardens. The grass and trees in Paris are so fresh, being constantly watered and great care bestowed on them. Now we are in the Champs Elysée and here it is like fairy land. Our destination is reached and we mount to the troisieme etage. The rooms vary from seven to twelve francs. Leaman the landlady said that the higher up the dearer. Mrs Sim said we prefer to descend in height and price! But the rooms are very pleasant and the table good. We dine at 6.30 and then go out and have a turn by the River, beautifully cool and pleasant. We walked round the Eiffel Tower and watched the coloured fountains.

Friday, 18thJuly. Took boat up the Seine to the Louvre. Magnificent collection of paintings - a gallery of Rubens and then a room of gems, the Salle Carré – Van Dyck, Murillo, Tintoretto, Salvator, Rosa, Van Eyck, Raphael, Holbein - we could spent a month here. We see jewellery and the Royal crown and many portraits. We are delighted with Paris and its wonderful sights. We then visit Bon Marché - an immense place. We bought presents and some decorations for ourselves. We also visited the Palais Royal and the Rue de Tivoli where there are some nice shops, but on the whole Regent Street is better for fine shops. We went up the Eiffel Tower – hurrah! The Hippodrome was our resort on Saturday night. Capital horsemanship and a little play Jeanne D'Arc. Carnot is there and the Marseillese [sic] is struck up. All stand.

Sunday morning we attend High Mass at the Madeline; fine music. After lunch we go to Notre Dame. We take the bateau up the river. Service just ending- beautiful music. Fine cathedral, the façade beautiful with rich carvings. We proceed to La Sainte Chapelle, a perfect gem of architecture, pure Gothic and exquisite windows. Now down the River to get a cab to Bois de Boulogne – lovely drive. Home just in time for dinner.

Monday, 21st July. Took the tram to the Boulevard St. Germain and find Hachettes for books. Then to the Magasin du Louvre. Opera in the evening, it is very fine – William Tell. I enjoy the singing immensely. The Ballet is very peaceful.

Tuesday, 22nd July. We left Paris by the evening train for Geneva. We are in a ladies' carriage. A French woman with a falsetto voice got in and did not cease to chatter all night. We did not sleep much. In the early morning the countryside was wonderful. A dim mist over all and in the distance mountains from which the veil of mist was gradually rising, revealing jagged rocks and peaks. Now we reach Geneva. We go to our Hotel, have a wash, then drink café au lait. We then find Mlle Bornet and with her we take a drive round Geneva and climb the Cathedral Tower. We visit an old Protestant church where Calvin preached his first sermon. We sit in his chair. Adjoining is a pretty little chapel, recently renovated - Chapel of the Rechabites. View from the tower beautiful, the Lake lying very peaceful at the foot of the hills and in the distance Mont Blanc towers in pure white among the fleecy clouds. We have tea with Madlle Bornet and then find ourselves on the steamer on Lake Geneva en route for Lausanne. Well has our poet Byron described the Lake Geneva:

> *Clear placid Leman*
> *This quiet sail is as*
> *A noiseless wing,*
> *To waft me from distraction.*
> *Once I loved torn ocean's roar*
> *But thy soft murmuring sounds sweet.*

May I say that I received a letter from home at Geneva Hotel and felt so joyful, all being well. Therefore I enjoyed the scenery all the more, the heights, the noble mountains, many being wooded up their sides.

We reach Lausanne, the town being hilly with many trees. We reach the Hotel Gibbon and are shown our rooms, they are charming, overlooking the Lake. There are beautiful gardens where Gibbon wrote his history. We take a walk.

Next day we leave for Interlaken – the views are beyond description. We cannot stop at any of the pretty villages, but get off at Berne for an hour. The lunch here was very dear. Sail up Lake Thun, very lovely. Stop at Lauterbrunnen to see Staubach - said to be the highest unbroken fall in Europe. Now back by rail to Zweilübchiner and have dinner at a funny inn, schap-braten, bran-toffeln and bier – 2m.50 each. We eat our dessert under a tree beside the stream. Now we proceed to Grindelwalt among the everlasting mountains with the valleys below and chalets dotted everywhere in the green slopes. We arrive and see two glaciers. We follow the path but are pestered by guides offering ponies, sedan chairs. We intend to go on foot. For an hour we follow a lovely path by hill and dale, some parts steep. As we descend we hear an Alpine horn and the sound of a cannon. The mountain before us is the Wetterhorn. The first sight of the glacier is disappointing, but as we approach it presents an object of peculiar interest. The air is cooling and the huge ice turrets and their bluish tint are remarkable. At last we are up and have to pay 50 centimes to go down to the Grotto. We are now on ice – big blocks, and above us tower fantastic shapes – pagoda-like structures. The grotto is cut into the glacier. We were really hot with climbing and as we entered the feeling of shock of the cold was intense. The clear ice cast a beautiful blue light over walls and ceiling. The effect was extraordinary. The grotto penetrated a considerable distance. The cold became more and more intense as we proceeded. We returned and had some tea which we enjoyed. We gathered some red flowers (unknown). The train took us back to Interlaken by 8.30. A long and exciting day.

Thursday, 23rd July. We leave for Lucerne at 11.25. This is a wonderful journey - for the first part the carriages are provided with an upper storey – pleasant, it being open all round. Now we sail over Lake Brienz to take a train over the mountains, now on one side then across to the other. Beautiful waterfalls without number. We ascend very high and very steep, the gradient is 700 per 1000 metres. Sometimes we simply crawl up. The views of the lakes, mountains, tarns surpasses all we have seen. We have a lively conversation with a nice German couple. We pass Mount Pilatus and here is the Riji. In Lucerne we take a walk – the houses remind me of pictures of Venice. The flora is very interesting- as we crawled along we saw many wild flowers, yellow foxglove, valerian and several plants we did not know. Edelweiss grows much higher, I believe, at about 8000 feet. We accomplished the ascent of the Kiji.

Friday, 24th July Started from Lucerne by steamer for one and a half hours. Then on we go by train. A funny little engine pushes its car, seating about 50 people, before it, and very slowly we jog along. The engine is provided with a cog-wheel, which catches every turn on a prepared rail in the centre of the Railroad. Some parts of the ascent are very steep. We look over the side of an awful defile, a wild stream below. Again we are on the edge of a precipice. At last after an hour and a half we are at the top, and see the wonder of wonders, a dense mist enveloping everything and so cold the wraps we brought being quite necessary. The mist somewhat cleared, we get glimpses of lovely scenery. We counted nine lakes but could not quite decipher the snowy mountains. After wandering around to see the different views we found the way to the station and descended – this time the engine goes in front. We made a mistake and took the wrong boat, and had to return. As a result we did not get to our hotel until 10 p.m.

From Lucerne we go to Schaffhausen to the Hotel Scweitzer Hof. It is beautifully situated overlooking the noble Rhine, the turbulent water rolling and leaping over huge boulders. We greatly enjoyed our walk.

29th July. It took us ten hours to get to Heidleberg. It is a quaint town; on the one side it rises abruptly on a high hill, on the other the hill on which is built an old and very beautiful castle. It is a famous town for wine, which is broached once a year, and with great rejoicing with quantities drunk and then re-filled with new wine.

Next day we began our journey towards the Rhine. We reached Basle and then Maintz and enjoyed this so much. We had dinner and tea aboard the boat and arrived at Coblenz at 8 o'clock. We had quite a tramp to the station and should have taken a cab. We then went on to Bonn where several Royal passengers got into the next carriage. No fuss was made, the students simply taking off their caps. They journeyed a short distance and got off at Brühl Castle. Now we reach Cöln at about midnight. We got a hearty welcome. Next day we went round the city and I saw the new part and the new Volks Garten. We went round the Cathedral which I know very well. It took 700 years to complete. The towers are 500 years old. We also visited the oldest church, we think, in the whole world – built in the year 400 A.D. This church is St Gereous and is built in the Moorish style. The renovation has been going on for eight years and will take 10 years more to complete. (The rest of this account deals with her happy reunion with friends she had made there ten years ago).

We left Cöln en route for Rotterdam, a weary journey, so hot and dusty. We felt quite done up. Some time to wait here. When we arrived at Amsterdam we were so relieved to find our ship, The Mascotte there. How we rejoiced. Leave our bags and go to a hotel to have dinner. On our way back we bought bulbs. Then a thunderstorm began and we hurried to get our tram. We asked our way but the Dutch language is a puzzle and beat us to understand or to make our wants known. Fortunately an Englishman came to the rescue and we reached our ship. We were glad to get aboard. What a grand terrific storm it was, the lightning so terribly vivid and forked. We had a nice calm voyage and no stoppage this time. Only I felt terribly done up and ill. Nellie too was obliged to give in and we lay very helpless.

Leith is reached and thus endeth a delightful month on holiday. I need not tell of the delights of home-coming nor the glad happy faces of the dear children, husband and friends.

I have transcribed this as best I can. It seems she wrote it whenever she could snatch a few minutes. Her descriptions move from past to present tense and back again. I am filled with admiration for the energy of Aunt Mina who was well over sixty. I note how carefully they watched what they spent, and how many friends they visited (I have omitted some of this).

I can imagine the children at Darliston when their mother returned. My mother was six, Ann was five, Gordon four and Charlie three. I would love to know what presents their mother brought back to them. And I am sure that their father would have read the diary with the greatest interest, particularly the part about Middlesborough as he himself was a shipowner. I do not know if they ever had a holiday abroad together after their honeymoon. They used to come and stay with us each year and we all spent some of the time at Scarborough. But I am running on into the third decade of the next century.

**Thomas Russell JP b.1863 (Elgin) d.1955 (Oamara), of Millburn
NZ m.25.10.1889 Catherine Jane Elizabeth Fleming 1865-1936** ch.
  1. Hulse Alexander Russell 1890-1891
  2. see below;
  3. Mary Jane Hulse Russell MB ChB b.1895
  4. Fleming Alexander Russell 1898-1920
  5. Catherine Margaret Anderson Russell b.1902 m.James Read

Tom Russell and his wife Catherine Fleming, New Zealand

6. Veda Tomina Russell b.1907 m. Lester J. Bain ch.
Russell Richard Bain b.1939 m.1944 Diana Jean Cunningham ch.

> (1) Andrew Russell Bain b.1973 (2) Angus Eden Bain b.1975

2. Albert Eden MBE 1892-1980 m.1923 Eileen Blanche McElrea b.1901 ch:

> **(1) Eileen Patricia Russell b.1924** m.1947 Allan Johnson (descendants)

> **(2) Vivienne Blanche Russell b.1925** m.6.9.1948 Edmond McLean 1922 ch.

> > 1. John Russell McLean b.1949 m.1972 Rosslyn Ethel Grey ch:

> > > (1) Jonathan Alan McLean b.1973 m. Bronwyn Collie ch.
> > > Jake Samuel McLean b.2003
> > > (2) Kate Frances McLean b.1975
> > > (3) Hamish Russell McLean b.1979

> > 2. Lindsay Robert McClean b.1952 m.1982 Susan Helen Edilson ch.

> > > (1) Timothy Mark McLean b.1985
> > > (2) Michael James McLean b.1985
> > > (3) Julia Irene McLean b.1987

> > 3. Jeremy James McLean b.1954 m.1982 Sandra Merle Rhind ch.

> > > (1) Sarah Ann McLean b.1985
> > > (2) Peter James McLean b.1987
> > > (3) Rebecca Mary McLean b.1987

> > 4. Dougal Russell McLean b.1967 m.1998 Catherine Frances Sparrow ch.

> > > (1) Emma Constance McLean b.1999
> > > (2) Sophie Frances McLean b.2000
> > > (3) Thomas Edmond McLean b.2002

(3) John Alexander Russell LLB b.1928 m.1955 Shirley
Margaret Bremner ch.

1. Philippa Jane Hulse Russell b.1957 m.1984 Stephen Lesley
   Heddles ch:
   (1) Jamie Stephen Heddles b.198
   (2) Keturah Jane Heddles b.1987
2. Maryanne Margaret Russell b.1963 m.4.5.1969 Russell
   Kroom ch.
   (1) Cameron Robert Kroom b.1997
   (2) Finlay Fletcher Kroom b.1999
3. Matthew John Eden Russell b.1965 m.1974 Louise Vereker-
   Binden ch:
   Gabrielle Morgan Russell b.2004
4. Simon Alexander James Russell b.1969

(4) Ruth Mary Russell b.1933 m.1956 Michael Henry
Buckenham ch.

1. Nicholas Ross Buckenham b.1957 m. 24.5.1987 (in
   Hawaii) Caroline Walker Schelley b.1961 ch.
   (1) Nicholas Walker Buckenham b.1996
   (2) Brian Edward Buckenham b.1998
2. Timothy Michael Buckenham b.1959 m.30.9. 93 Sabina
   Josephine Noonan (at Edinburgh) ch:
   (1) Henry Finbar Buckenham b.1995
   (2) Lucy Hugo Buckenham b.1997 d.y.
   (3) Millie Skye Buckenham b.1998
   (4) Scarlett Fenella Buckenham b.2001
3. Sally Ruth Buckenham b.1963 m.13.3.1993 Peter Garth
   Boyle b.1963 ch:
   (1) Alexander Buckenham Boyle b.1995
   (2) Emily Buckenham Boyle b.1998
   (3) Timothy Buckenham Boyle b.2000
4. Susan Belinda Buckenham b.10.11.1966

CHART G: ABBREVIATED CHART OF THE ADAM FAMILY

These are details from the chart, which are relevant to the story of my book. The Adam ancestors of Birnie and the McKessack (with various spellings of the name) of Pluscarden have been traced to the early 18th century.

William Adam b. of Barden and Kinnedar 1804 (d.1892)
m.14.5.1840 Ann Hardy McKessack 1815 at Crossley, Pluscarden ch:
  1. **Jessie Adam 1842-1888** (see below)
  2. Charles Adam 1845-1887 MD in Elgin for 50 years unm.
  3. James Adam 1845-1887 Westfield
  4. **William Gordon Adam 1847-1930 Burghead and Elgin m. Keturah Russell** (see Chart H, Chapter 10)
  5. John Adam 1849-1938 unm.
  6. **Jane Hardy Adam (Jeannie) 1851-1939** (see below)
  7. Alexander Adam 1853-1933 Kineddar m. Mary King
  8. Robert Adam b.1855 farmer in Essex
  Annie Adam b.1857 m. John Farquhar
  10. **Marjorie Riach Adam 1859-1915** (see below)
  11. Twins who died young in 1859

Details of 1. above:
Jessie Adam m. 15.5.1875 John Tulloch 1835-1892 ch:
  1. William David Tulloch 1876-1942 m. Susan Hendry MA Hons (William and Susan had six surviving children, four of whom had descendants)
  2. James Hendry Tulloch b.1921 (Dyke) d.2001 (Thurlow, Suffolk) m.1946 Doreen Alcock, Staffs. (he farmed at Gt Wratting Suffolk) ch:

one son Alistair James Hendry Tulloch b.1950 m.1977
Rosemary Ann Rowe ch:
(1) James Alexander Tulloch 1983
(2) Christopher Robert Tulloch 1986 (Cheveley
Newmarket)

Details of 6. above:

**Jane Hardy Adam m.30.6.1881 William Robertson b.1821, Mains
of Aberlour and Linkwood ch:**

1. Elspeth Grant Robertson b.1883 m. T.B. Philips
2. Colin Robertson d. in infancy
3. William Adam Robertson b.1887 m. Selma Olsen (Victoria
B.C.) no ch.
4. Annie (Nan) Robertson b.1899 unm.
5. Alexander Grant (Sandy) Robertson 1890-1972 m. Helen
Poore, London ch:
(1) Jane Anne Robertson m. Harold Anderson (Kingston)
ch:
Janet Anderson, Susan Anderson, Alexander
Anderson (line continues)
(2) Sandra Madge Robertson m. C.B. (Brad) Schneller
(Missuaga) ch:
Ann Elizabeth Schneller b.1967,
David Schneller b.1968
6. Dorothea (Dora) Robertson 1892-1952 unm.
7. Mabel Grant Robertson b.1893 m. Dr Gordon Thow,
Elgin no ch.
8. Ian Stephen Robertson b.1895 m.1919 Helen (Ellie) Reid
ch:
(1)   Neil Robertson b.1921 Linkwood m. Marie Young
ch:
Alison Joan Robertson b.1949, Joan Robertson
b.1950, Moira Robertson b.1951, Ian Robertson

b.1958, Elizabeth Robertson b.1962 (line continues)
(2) Bruce Robertson b.1924 m.1953 Edith Barker ch:
   Catriona Robertson
(3) Shiela Rosemary Robertson b.1929 m. Douglas
   Williamson (Sudbury) ch:
   Susan Elizabeth Williamson b.1955
   Alexander Williamson b.1958
9. Colin Grant Robertson 1926-27

Details of 10. above:
**Marjorie Riach Adam m.1916 William Grant 1849-1915 solicitor
ch:**
   Eight children; the 7th child: Marjory Anne Grant b.1918 m.
   Harold M.J. Westcott 1920-1968 ch:
   1. Elizabeth Anne Wescott b.1946 m. Tim Sheffield ch: Susan
      Sarah Sheffield b.1970
   2. Shiela Margaret Westcott b.1947 m. Kem Majid 2 children

CHAPTER 10

THREE FAMILY PHOTOGRAPHS

The first family photograph was taken in the summer of 1895. Mother and Father and the six children had been placed in position, and had instructions to sit quite still. All was set, but action had to be postponed for a minute as the photographer popped his face out from under the black hood and said, "Ready. Now all of you watch just here for the dicky bird". This made Charlie laugh and that set them all off. There was a delay while Father spoke firmly to the children, and in response they addressed the matter in hand with due solemnity. Russell, the youngest of the family and the delight of them all, is seated on his father's knee. He is wearing shoes, so must have been able to stand. On his left is Ann, blue-eyed and golden- haired and wearing an elaborate dress. Mother's blouse is so smart that I wish it had been a legacy to me. Wilfred is seated on her right, his dear gentle face quite grave, though we all remember him as full of fun and jokes. The two older boys, Gordon (front left) and Charlie, still smiling, wear kilts and jackets. Mary, my mother, stands at the back wearing her new dress, a grand dress with a bolero and fichu. And the name of the family dog, who knew how to behave, was Bruce. Mary looks as if she were as good as gold. – but occasionally she slipped. She told me about a trick she played on her sister Ann. One evening, when they were in bed, she said to her,

"You must behave, because I have eyes in the back of my head, so I can always see what you are up to". Ann replied that she did not believe it.

"All right, I'll prove it", Mary said. "I will go and sit on the chair beside the window with my back to you. We must not put on the light

The Adam Family at Darliston, c.1895: back row (L-R) Mary, Mother; middle row (L-R) Gordon, Charlie, Father with Russell on his knee, Wilfred; front row Ann, Bruce the dog

in case Mother comes up. When I call, you get out of bed, feel your way over, put your hands out and I will guide them to the eyes at the back of my head."

Mary seated herself facing forward, and put her long hair over her face. She took Ann's hands and guided them to the mysterious eyes. Ann screamed, and up came Mother, and there was trouble. But then Mother saw the funny side and began to laugh. She appreciated pranks as much as anyone, and calmed Ann and had her laughing too. From the photograph it seems to be a prosperous family. Running the business at Burghead was arduous, and William Adam's position on the Council was not always a smooth ride. From the *Northern Scot*, of 17 May 1887 we have the following: at a meeting at Burghead called by the residents, an address was read and presented to Mr William Adam.

"We the residents of Burghead wish to give our thanks to you for what you have done. In the face of much opposition, and latterly of not a little personal abuse, you were instrumental both in procuring for us a supply of water, and in furthering the amenity of our dwelling place by a system of drainage. You have also done what lay in your power to lighten the parochial burdens weighing so heavily on the householders of this parish, and have ever kept a jealous eye over the expenditure of public money with the view to obtaining as strict economy as was consistent with efficiency.

Recognising these your public acts, as well as your disinterested kindness to the poor, and your maintenance as a pure and honourable man, we, the inhabitants of Burghead, in public meeting assembled beg you to accept this address as a token of our gratitude for what you have hitherto done, and as an index of our sympathy for you in your recent troubles, and we venture to express the hope that these will be surmounted and that your further endeavours for the people of Burghead will be successful."

After applause Mr Adam thanked them and acknowledged in the matter of the drainage the support he had been given by Messrs Wink, Jenkins, Niven and Ross and he thanked those who had "put their hands in their pockets". He said "I have been looking at the death rate, and found that since the introduction of the water it had fallen consistently in Burghead. Before we had the present supply the death rate was 27 or 28 per thousand. In a few years after we had got water it had fallen to twenty two, and now we have got the place properly drained I believe it must be as low as 18 to 20."

He went on to his plans to continue to lower the taxation on water. He ended, "The present public expression of sympathy is very pleasing to me, and to those connected with me, and in my and their name I once more thank you very sincerely for the address presented to me."

Six years later another setback had to be faced and surmounted. *The Northern Scot* of 25 November 1893 describes the tragic loss of one of William Adam's ships.

Wreck of a Burghead Vessel – All Hands Lost

The most serious wreck took place 16 miles west of Banff on Saturday morning. The fishermen of Sandsend, while attending to the moorings of their boats, found pieces of wreckage floating ashore near the harbour. And this was the first intimation that on the bleak and rocky headland a mile distant a wreck had taken place. On the day dawning the whole shore for several miles was strewn with wood, steering gear, doors of lockers, panelling and other appurtenances of a large steamer. Among the wreckage washed up was a clock which had stopped at quarter to twelve o'clock. And there was also found the keels of two ship's boats showing that the crew had taken to the boats as a last resource. An important piece of evidence relating to the identity of the wrecked ship was a spar of wood with the word MORAY branded on it. It is believed that the Steamer is the Moray belonging to Mr William Adam, chemical manufacturer, Burghead, which was principally engaged on the coal trade between Sunderland and Burghead. The Moray left Burghead going down the Firth on Thursday, and about eleven o'clock on Friday night, when the storm was about at its height, a light was seen off the point of Sandsend, and a steamer's whistle was heard. The Moray was a steel screw three masted steamer, 438 tons gross, and of 60 horse power engines. She was built in September 1889 by the Grangemouth Dockyard Company at Alloa and engined by Allen and M'Lennan, Glasgow.

It is now surmised that the vessel foundered without touching the rocks, and went to the bottom just off Garron Point, and that the boilers burst and blew up the after-cabin, the hull remaining intact. Had she struck the rocks, the vessel, it is believed, would have been dashed to pieces, and the cargo would have thrown up soon after. We understand the vessel and its cargo were insured The Captain of the vessel was J. Macnamara. The names of the crew on board the Moray at the time of the disaster were – Wm.Winchester (40), master, Buckie, married, resides in Aberdeen; first mate, name unknown, joined at Hartlepool on previous voyage; James Drummond, (32), chief engineer, Arbroath, married; John Stewart (65), cook, Fraserburgh, married; John Kreft (30), A.B. Germany; J. Brahm (28) A.B.;- Hutcheson (60) A.B., Orkney; James M'Arthur, fireman, (30), Burghead unmarried; George Reid, fireman (23), Burghead,

Duncan Adam of Glassgreen, Elgin, with anchor of 'The Moray'
*(*Northern Scot, 10 April 1996*)*

unmarried; R. Jack, fireman (23), Charlestown, Fife; second
engineer, name unknown, joined ship at Sunderland.

I have quoted this almost in full as an excellent piece of reporting, and
as typical of so many tragedies of this sort that occurred up and down
the coasts of Scotland. The loss of 'The Moray' must have been blow
to William Adam, but not nearly so severe to him as the loss of a final
count of thirteen men.

But life at Darliston was pleasant and equable. Tudy and William
had similar backgrounds and got on very well together. On the
Sabbath the whole family went to St Giles for the morning service,
filling the Adam pew. The service was lengthy but the children were
well disciplined, except for one Sunday when there was an incident at
church, just before the service was about to start. Tudy was wearing a
bonnet, which was decorated with ornaments and net. A friend who
was sitting in the pew in front was wearing a similar bonnet. She
turned round, and she and Tudy were exchanging some whispered
news, their heads close together. Somehow the ornaments became
enmeshed and William had to come to the rescue and disentangle the
two ladies. Charlie began to laugh and all the children followed.
Father was stern, but they continued to heave with painful
suppression.

This episode was not nearly so grave as a dispute which arose
between Tudy and William. William obtained a copy of Charles
Darwin's *Origin of the Species* and read it avidly. After much
deliberation he made a grave announcement to his wife. He declared
that scientifically and logically Darwin's theory fitted all the evidence,
and that it answered all the many queries and doubts which arose in
those parts of the bible which seemed unacceptable, and to be merely
folk tales. This meant that he felt he was now unable to attend church.
Of course Tudy was very upset, but treated the matter as if it was a
temporary aberration. She was hopeful that one Sunday morning her
husband would waken to his old faith. The older children were aware

of all this. Mary (my mother) told us that on Sunday mornings they used to tiptoe along to their parents' room and listen at the door. One time they heard Tudy say

"But William, people are talking. Will you not, for my sake, just attend church this Sunday?"

"My dear Tudy," he said, "I cannot act against my principles. It would be sheer hypocrisy. How could I listen to such words as 'God made the Heaven and Earth and all that in them is in seven days'?"

"And how can you, William, believe that we human beings are descended from apes, and not made by the Creator of all?"

When the family grew up, Wilfred was the only one who regularly went to church, but I think my mother might have attended if there had been a Presbyterian Church in the village where she lived after her marriage.

As for my dear Uncle Wilfred and his family, who have remained close to my mother and to us, I will write a little more fully about them, so that I can go forward in time and complete the story of the wreck of 'The Moray'. After Wilfred left Elgin Academy, went into an architect's office and trained as a surveyor. Then he decided to emigrate to Canada, and was there for the next twenty three years. He worked at various jobs: he delivered coal down the coal chutes to the furnaces in the basements of the houses. He worked on the building of the Grand Treeak Railway. He surveyed the first road up to Lake Wasakesui north of the P.A. For part of that time he lived in Prince Albert, Saskatchewan. When the Great War broke out he joined the Saskatchewan Regiment of the Canadian Army. I will write more of that later. On return to Canada he farmed in the bush near Port Albert. On 10 October 1928 Wilfred was married to Isobella Duncan Thomson at Montreal. They honeymooned at the Niagara Falls (as his parents had!) 'Isbe' Thomson came from Elgin; her father farmed Glassgreen. Wilfred and Isbe had two children, Duncan John (1929) and Mary Elizabeth (1932).

Uncle Wilfred seemed to be able to turn his hand to anything and always with success. In the winter he cut ice on the Saskatchewan River. The ice was stored in the Ice Barn to be delivered all the summer to the houses for the iceboxes. Latterly Wilfred teamed up with a Mr Carr and started the Northern Cartage Company. This, through Wilfred's management skills, flourished. His daughter Mary, who now lives in Twassan B.C., writes that she still sees the wagons with the company name on them.

In 1935 Wilfred, Isbe and the children returned to Elgin. Isbe's mother, Mrs Thomson, had died, and they came back to help Isbe's father. I know how delighted our Granny Adam at 24 Hay Street was to see these grandchildren for the first time and to have them living nearby. Wilfred farmed Glassgreen with all his skills. As a citizen of Elgin he was an admirable successor to his father William Adam and to his grandfather Alexander Russell. He became an elder at St Giles in 1947. He was a member of the Board of Governors of Anderson's, serving for quite a number of years as Chairman. He served on both the Moray County Council and the Moray and Nairn County Council for twenty-five years. Isbe died in 1980; Wilfred lived to be 91. One short story will show his spirit. It was harvest time and Wilfred had spent the morning at the Farmer's Mart. After lunch he went out to the fields and boarded the combine harvester. Time passed so Duncan went out to the fields to find him. "Father, it's time you came in and had a rest, you've been on the go all day." With an astonished look Wilfred said, "What? I've done NOTHING. Just talking this morning, and sitting this afternoon."

The story of Glassgreen must be similar to that of many farming families in Scotland. Duncan grew up with farming in his blood. He went to Strathallan School and then to Aberdeen University, and on 30 October 1954 was married to Dorothy Jeanie Sleigh, daughter of an Aberdeenshire farmer, and physiotherapist at Gray's Hospital. I was at the wedding, which took place in Kings College Chapel, Aberdeen. In preparation for this marriage, and for Wilfred's retirement, a spacious bungalow had been built at the bottom of the drive to the

'Big House' as it was called. So Dorothy and Duncan began their married life in the 'Big House'.

When I visited Elgin in 1979 I arrived at Wilfred's bungalow and had the usual warm welcome, and then Uncle Wilfred said excitedly, "I've got a new washing machine, you must see it." I wondered why it pleased him so much. He led me to the bathroom and right in the centre of the floor was a large glass hut containing a shower and a seat! "This is my personal washing machine," he said. "I got stuck in the bath the other night."

We can now turn back to the story of the loss of 'The Moray', with an article from the *Northern Scot* of 10 April 1996.

Anchor Surfaces from long-lost Moray Wreck

While diving in the waters off Sandsend, a Portknockie man, Mr Brian Donaldson, found the wreck of one of the Moray boats lost during the Great Gale of 1893. After carrying out some research he pieced together enough information to discover that the boat belonged to the grandfather of Elgin farmer Mr Duncan Adam. Mr Adam of Glassgreen was taken aback when contacted by Mr. Donaldson out of the blue, and to hear that he had discovered the wreckage of "The Moray". He was well aware of the boat's tragic fate, as its 13-man crew was lost when "The Moray" went down. Asked if he would like a token of remembrance from the wreckage, Mr Adam asked if it would be possible to raise the anchor. Although raising the anchor had been quite a complicated business requiring the use of air bags, Mr Adam took delivery of the piece of family history about a fortnight ago.

The photograph on Page 140 shows the anchor, and in the background of this photo are the steadings, which in the course of time held calves, then piglets, then day-old chicks. It has always been a joy to go to Glassgreen, whether to the Big House or the Bungalow. We now take the chance to complete to date this part of the story. In 1991 James, Duncan and Dorothy's second son, and the successor to the farm, was married to Sarah. The marriage took place in the garden of Glassgreen. James' older brother Sandy, his wife Anne and their two sons were there. Sandy farmed at Craigellachie for some years and is now a prominent businessman in Elgin.

It wasn't Musical Chairs but Musical Houses. In their turn Duncan and Dorothy moved into the bungalow, and the young couple into the Big House. And in time there were grandchildren for Duncan and Dorothy, the eldest a baby girl, her name Keturah. Keturah has two brothers, Charlie and Duncan. It is good to see the family naming pattern, a long held tradition.

Having run ahead in time so that I could relate the story of wreck, I now have to return to 1904 to a serious setback in the fortunes of the happy Adam family of Darliston. For some time Keturah had been worried about her husband's health. He worked long hours. She arranged for a woman at Burghead to prepare a hot meal for him for mid-day, but after a short time she found out that he had terminated the arrangement, saying he could not spare the time. Eventually he had to agree to see the doctor. William Adam was diagnosed as having pulmonary tuberculosis and Keturah was told that there was little hope. However Tudy and William and William's brothers, one of whom was a doctor, and the rest of the family set to work and came to this conclusion: he would be nursed at home. Mary (my mother) came home to help with the nursing. The current methods in use in the sanatoria in Switzerland were to be adopted. William Adam was among the first to be given the new drug tuberculin, but as he was so weak he was given a dosage at half strength. The others in the group of patients who were given the drug all died. As an essential part of the treatment was fresh air, the windows were taken out of the main bedroom. The patient was kept warm and was on a diet of nourishing foods. As for the Works at Burghead, William agreed that he would not worry. He had confidence in a young man (his surname was Adam but he was not related), whom he had employed and trained as manager. The Adam brothers agreed to keep an eye on things. Keturah was always optimistic, cheering and serene. Against all the odds William recovered fully.

But there was unexpected trouble to face. The Burghead business was in chaos. The young manager had embezzled a large sum of money and left a list of outstanding debts. It was a bitter blow; in the final reckoning with the accountants it seemed that the firm would be bankrupt. My grandfather, with Keturah at his side, faced the matter with a determination and courage typical of him. He vowed that every debt would be paid. This would entail the unthinkable – the sale of their home, Darliston. What was the situation with regard to the children? Mary had gone back to Glasgow to continue her secretarial training. This she did most successfully and obtained the post of secretary to the Medical Superintendent of Woodielea, a big mental hospital near Bishopbriggs. Gordon was studying science at Christ College, Oxford. Ann had already left to visit the New Zealand Russells with the idea of settling there. Charlie hoped to emigrate to Canada, and Wilfred and Russell were still at school. What was to become of the younger ones? And here comes the wonderful family spirit, the rallying around of all the relatives. How hard it must have been for Keturah and William to ask for, and to take, such help.

I have one short letter which has been kept over all these long years. Nothing else can bring alive so clearly what my Grandparents suffered and how helpful all the relatives were. The notepaper has a printed address at the top.

TURVAR,
28, COURT ROAD,
W. NORWOOD, S.E
31.8.06.

My Dear Keturah,

What can I say to convey to you how very, very grieved we are to hear all you say. Keturah dear you have been a brave and courageous woman in the past so you must keep up your heart.

God is Great and Good. Now that things are on the way of being settled you will have peace of mind, which is indeed a great thing.

But it does all seem so hard just now. Asking me to lend Gordon a helping hand in a very small way is not begging, never let such a word pass between us. Mac is to see if anything he has can be turned to account, it will be well. With very great pleasure I'll send 3 flannel shirts to Gordon. He might say what he would like and the size of neck. Surely the uncles will bear a helping hand especially the Bachelor ones, putting Charlie in a good way and helping their brother.

I must catch the post. I did not notice it is so late. We are having very hot and very trying weather.

With kindest sympathy and much love

Yours affectionately,

Agnes J. Christisson

I'll write soon again. If you are selling your fruit and like to send me a barrel of apples at the retail price I'd be glad.

{To Tulse Hill Station, London,Brighton and South Coast Ry}

Well, the time came when there was peace of mind. Every debt was settled. For two years the Adams lived in rented houses, but then they were able to buy 24 Hay Street, in the same area as Darliston. Gordon did well in his university course, and was then employed by the Gas, Coke and Light Company. He was to have a very successful career. Charlie was hoping to emigrate to Canada. This he did in 1908, and shortly went to the Queen Charlotte Islands. He became Postmaster of Queenstown on 5 May 1912. Later he established a town site called Graham Centre where he ran a General Store. The place was quite successful but the war came and he joined up in 1916. When he returned he found his place had burnt to the ground. He then went to Stewart B.C. where he had a Ford dealership and also ran a taxi service. In the early 1940s he moved to Terrace B.C. and there set up a cinema, which filled a real need.

Russell, with the help of one of his uncles, was educated at Fettes College, Edinburgh. Ann liked New Zealand and obtained a teaching post at a Girls' School. She then met Walter Moore, a doctor in Napier

147

who ran his own private nursing home, and she became engaged to him. Before she married she came home to visit her parents, and en route visited her brothers in Canada. Charlie was living in what she considered 'the wilds'. His housekeeper had left, and he mentioned to her that he had saved up his washing and hoped she would do it for him. It was in a small hut; there was a very large pile. She thought it was beyond redemption, made a large bonfire and burnt it all! She went on to Elgin and then returned to marry Walter. Sadly the marriage was unsuccessful and short-lived, and she went back to her teaching post.

This chapter ends on a happy note in with the wedding of my mother, Mary Adam, the eldest of the family, in July 1913. Up to now, when they left school generations of girls settled at home to 'help mother', and wait hopefully for 'Mr Right' to come along. The Suffrage movement opened the way for careers for women. Mary and Ann benefited from this. The girls had been well educated at a private girls' school in Sydenham, London. All I remember my mother saying about the school was that the girls thoroughly enjoyed the concerts at the Crystal Palace. (I remembered her telling about this when many years later I was in London, and on the night of 30 November – 1 December 1936, was out for the evening at Blackheath. We saw the sky lit up a fearsome red. Next day I learned that this was the terrible Crystal Palace fire.)

Mary obtained the post of Secretary to the Medical Superintendent of Woodielea, a big Mental hospital near Bishopbriggs, Glasgow. Here she met William Anderson, a young medical student who was on a course there. William came from Lenzie in Ayrshire; he was tall, fair, blue-eyed - and of course handsome. They fell in love and became engaged. After William graduated, he went to Sunderland, County Durham, to work as assistant in the practice of his brother John. John was nearly twenty years older than Will, and when John was a medical student at Glasgow University and came home for weekends, Will used to say. "Here's the man with the wee suitcase." Will must have worked very hard, and perhaps had some financial help from his parents. After his time in Sunderland, Will joined Dr T.E. Ferguson as assistant in the practice of Dr Mark Wardle of Bishop Auckland and Coundon, in south west Durham. In 1912 William Anderson bought the Coundon practice, and Tom Ferguson took over the Bishop Auckland practice of Dr Ellis. The Ferguson and Anderson families have remained good friends up to the present time.

The Coundon area was partly mining and partly agricultural. There was an old farmhouse on the east edge of Coundon. A builder called Hetherington bought this, demolished it and built a new house which my father rented, and subsequently bought. As the house looked out to the Cheviot hills and to Roseberry Topping it was named Roseberry. The yard at the back of the house was the old farmyard and some of the buildings remained. A surgery was built adjacent to the house. Later my father bought the field in front so that it could not be built on, and rented it to a farmer. As children we watched the sowing of the corn in spring and the harvesting in the late summer.

Will and Mary's wedding was arranged for 12 July 1913. It was a great family gathering. Tudy was conscious, when she and Mary make the list for the invitations, that her side of the family was greatly outnumbered by the Adams. How sad Tudy was that her Mama at Queen's Street had died seven years ago. How pleased Mama would have been to see Mary 'safely and happily married'. Russell was at home, having left school and about to begin his training in Elgin as a banker. His objective was to work in a bank in the Far East. In the wedding photograph, taken outside Amberley, the house of Keturah's half brother Alick Russell and his wife, we see Mary's parents, her brother Russell and a galaxy of Adam relatives – her Linkwood Robertson and Grant cousins, her Uncle Alick, Kineddar, two generations of the Leitches, her Uncle Charles Adam. The men are in the back and centre rows, and the ladies in the front row. The bride's cousins May Leitch and Mabel Robertson were bridemaids. There were only two of the Merson family, Aunt Mina and Aunt Jessie. A happy day for all, I am sure.

The only member of William Anderson's family who was able to be there was his youngest sister Jean. The Best Man was Johnny Boyd, an old college friend. Will Anderson was a shy young man, and on a previous visit to Elgin had been overwhelmed by the number and style of Mary's relatives. I think that the wedding was an ordeal for him. I look at the bride's veil with interest, because I wore it at my wedding! Tudy looks so young, so neat and smartly dressed. And so that day began another chapter in the lives of my family.

CHART H: ABBREVIATED CHART OF THE FAMILY OF WILLIAM ADAM AND KETURAH RUSSELL

William Gordon Adam 1847-1930 m.19.7.1882 Keturah Elizabeth Russell 1851-1945 ch:

1. **Mary Gordon Adam 1884-1955 m.1913 Dr William Grieg Anderson** (see end of Chart J, Chapter 11) **ch:**
   (1) Elizabeth Cameron Anderson b.12.12.1915 m.1937 Rex Willsher
   (2) John Russell Anderson b.31.5.1918 m.1956 Audrey Margaret Shaw Wilson
   (3) Maryan Gordon Anderson b.11.2.1923 m.12.4.1964 John Huntridge, Cambridge
   (For families of the above, see Chart K, Chapter 12)
2. Ann Adam 1885-1970 m. (1) 1913 Dr Walter Moore, Napier, NZ m. (2) 1954 Leonard Sutherland, 1882-1957
3. William Gordon Adam 1886-1969 m.1922 Mabelle Olive Cerise Thorne d.1956
4. Charles Merson Adam 1887-1973 m.1952 'Susie' Hiench b.1912
5. **William Alfred (Wilfred) Adam 1892-1983 m.1928 Isbella Duncan Thomson 1894-1980**
6. Alexander Russell Adam 1895-1917

Children of 5. above:

1. **John Duncan Adam of Glassgreen 1929-1999 m. 1954 Dorothy Sleigh b.1929 ch:**
    (1) Alexander William (Sandy) Adam b.1956 m. Anne Dixon ch:
        1. Gordon Duncan Adam b.1983
        2. Scott Duncan Adam b.1985
    (2) Margaret Isabella Adam b.1958 m. David Rae ch:
        1. Callum Duncan Rae b.1986
        2. Donald Duncan Rae b.1989
    (3) James Gordon Adam b.1971 m. Sarah NcNab ch:
        1. Keturah Ann Adam b.1998
        2. Duncan Adam 1999
        3. Charles Adam

Mary Elizabeth Adam b.1932 m. 1966 Hugo Laanela 1926-2003 ch:
    Alexander Alan Laanela b.10.1.1967 Darwin, Australia m. Joanne ch (born Victoria, Vancouver):
        1. Ari Laanela b.2001
        2. Tia Keturah Michelle Laanela b.20.5.2003
    (2) Michael Adam Laanela b.10.1.1967 Darwin
    (3) Erica Elizabeth Laanela b.6.9.1971 Townsville, Australia

Wedding of Mary Adam and Dr William Anderson, July 1913

The Bride, the Bridegroom; the Best Man Johnnie Boyd; the Bridesmaids:
(L) Nellie Leitch, (R) Mabel Robertson

Mary Gordon Adam

At Roseberry, the new baby Betty and her parents

CHAPTER 11

MARY AND WILL ANDERSON

What did my mother think of the mining village of Coundon? I can only answer this by looking at the scene through my own eyes, my memories of things she told me. So I should mention that I, Elizabeth Cameron Anderson, was born on 12 December 1915, my brother John Russell on 31 May 1918 and our sister Maryan Gordon on 14 February 1923. We were all born at home.

Coundon was so very different from Elgin. Roseberry was 200 yards off the main street. Across that street there were neat rows of colliery houses named Tyne Tees, Esk, Wear. The front row faced south onto the road; and then the houses ran back to back. Each had a walled yard, with an 'ash privy', washing lines, and a tin bath which hung on the brick wall. There were front and back doors, but the front doors were rarely used. To the west of this large housing estate was the Eden Pavilion, erected in 1912 and a gift from Sir William and Lady Eden, a family whose estate was three miles away. The Pavilion's claim to fame was that a touring company came to perform and the player who received enormous applause was the young Charlie Chaplain. It was in this Pavilion (our Picture House), with its downstairs penny (or a jam jar) and two-penny seats for the Saturday matinees, that we children saw some of the great old cowboy films. Occasionally our whole family went in the early evening. We had one of the two boxes, and we were provided with a high chair for our dog who attentively followed the film, waiting for the appearance of one of his own kin, or better still a cat. He would then bark, but briefly, and the audience would laugh and clap.

The main street, Collingwood Street, had a few essential shops, most of them in the front room of the owners' houses, with the door and passage incorporated. 'The Browns' was our corner shop; Mrs Brown ran it and Mr Brown and his sons farmed the fields around our house. It was our sweetie shop where we spent our Saturday pennies on gob-stoppers, liquorice bootlaces and such delights. There was Fishwick's, the paper shop, which also sold yeast. The yeast was in a sacking bag and was served by using a scoop. Everyone bought yeast there for the bread and teacake bakings; I was filled with delight when for the first time I was asked if I would 'run a message and fetch tuppence worth of yeast'.

We always hurried past the dentist's surgery. Mr Staveley did a good trade with brides-to-be; so bad was the rate of tooth decay that it was fashionable for brides-to-be to have all their teeth extracted and appear with a gleaming set of dentures in good time for the wedding. There was a fruit and vegetable shop owned and run by a Miss Hilda M——, who made an unfortunate marriage with a philanderer – 'a wide boy' they called him in the pub. I think that it was three times that he took the money from the till, and 'went off with a blonde'. He soon returned, penitent, and was forgiven. Friends advised Martha to make a stand, which she did, saw him off, and to compensate for her loss she bought a Hillman Minx and learned to drive. Then Theresa, our faithful maid, told my mother that the worst had happened. Hilda had taken him back. When they had remonstrated with her she replied, "It's all very well to say that, but ye canny sleep with a Hillman Minx."

There was the Corn Shop kept by Mr Shortland, who stocked all sorts of cereals in bins. There was Kidd's the Chemist; Billy Kidd was a friend of my father and they shared interests in backing horses and in football. Mr Manners the butcher sold first-class meat; he soon adapted to the names and types of cuts of meat which my Scottish mother required. The Sunday joints at Roseberry are unforgettable. The shop known as Kells was owned by a Mr Kell, and his three grown-up daughters served and did the work in it. The left half was a sweetie shop, and on Saturdays my father stocked up for the week: mintoes, Dainty Dinah toffees, and very occasionally chocolate bars. The other half of 'Kells Shop' was a drapers; ladies and gents socks, stockings, underwear, etc. The time came when one of the three sisters was married. But she was soon back home and enquiring customers were told, "Oh married life didn't suit our Mary, and it's just lovely to get her back with us." I remember going in to buy something and asking how they all were, as I knew they had had flu. The answer was, "Me mum and our dad is on the mend, our Jane'll soon be up, and even Polly's rallied."

I do not remember a baker's shop until later on; every household did its own baking. The Co-op was a general store, but my mother did a weekly shopping in Bishop Auckland, one of the main objectives being Lipton's, or the Kings Hall lending library, or the fascinating Spoors' Ironmongery. Until after the First World War my mother used to travel to what was usually called 'Bishop' in the local pony and trap, and after that she took the bus. She enjoyed shopping; she enjoyed chatting with the local people and became well liked. She was helpful to those who were ill. She began a regular evening meeting in our house for the 'Girls Friendly Society'. My father called it the 'Girls Bickering Club'. Initially my mother was pleased with Roseberry, later she longed for an older, larger house and twice was very disappointed when deals fell through. But in the early days there was plenty of space: two large bedrooms at the front looking east; two smaller ones to the west, one of which was the maids' room. Until after the 1939 war was over we always had two maids who were very much part of the family. Downstairs there was a sitting room and a dining room, the kitchen with its cooking stove, and a room which became the nursery. In the evenings the maids sat in comfortable chairs with the stove door open and a cheerful furnace in view. There were blazing fires in the rooms in those early days, and tons of coal were delivered to the coal-house in the yard. The coal cart was drawn by a horse, as was the dust-cart which came to empty rubbish. The household waste had its own brick house with a high up door from the washhouse and a low door outside in the yard. It was called the ash-pit. My parents once had a long discussion about my brother John. He must have been about six or seven, and they decided he needed to play with other boys. So two or three were invited to come and play in the garden. It swiftly became a gang of six or so. In the absence of our parents and the gardener John inaugurated a Follow-my-Leader game. He prepared the course: opened the front door, the kitchen back door and the two little doors of the ash-pit were opened. The string of followers rampaged through flowerbeds, climbed up on a wall and onto a roof, and raced through the vegetable garden Then John led them to the front door and through the house into the washhouse. He led the way headfirst through the high door of the rubbish-house to slide down and emerge in the yard. It was a great adventure, but quite understandably a ban was put on the game.

Coundon air was polluted by the Leasingthorne coal mine workings, and my mother was amazed to find that the net curtains in the front rooms had to be washed every other week. After my parents bought the house they made several alterations. A seriously large pantry was built on at the east side. I recall the long marble shelves, a strange net tent under which the joint was kept, and rows and rows of pots of jam and jelly and marmalade and bottled fruits. From time to time relatives of my mother came to stay. The pantry is associated in my mind with a visit by a cousin of my mother's, Madge Grant from Elgin. She had married an engineer, John Taylor, and they had emigrated to Canada. Madge came home on a visit and brought her two little girls to stay with us. I remember one incident very clearly. After we had all been put to bed, our young visitors persuaded us to 'raid the pantry and have a midnight feast'. By sitting at the top of the stairs we were able to assess the right moment for the raid. The dining room door was closed; we came down and tiptoed past it. Once in the pantry we loaded up two plates with cold potatoes, bits of chicken and cakes. The feast was held a long time before midnight. I recall a feeling of elation mixed with guilt. Next day we were taken to the photographers in Bishop Auckland; the photographer produced a picture of children with angelic looks!

When my Mother's uncle John Adam in Elgin died, he left a sum of money to each of his brother's children, and with this my mother fulfilled one of her dreams. A fine sunroom was built on the south side of the house, opening out from the dining room. The view down the garden was pleasing, but had been ruined for years as my father had a large ex-army hut erected there as a billiard house. There was a gas fire at each end and Dad greatly enjoyed having his friends to play. My mother made use of it when she held jumble sales there. For many years the miners' families were living in poverty. The children often went barefoot and without coats. She recognised that the people did not want charity, that they had their pride. She collected piles of clothes from friends, and advertised the sale in the shops. Word flew round. On the morning of the sale there was always a long queue, then when the door was opened a scramble, and the table was soon absolutely cleared.

My mother set to work at once on the garden; it was a major interest which my parents shared. To the east there was a bare-looking wooden fence. A row of poplar trees was planted, also a privet hedge and a sycamore tree. They all flourished. Everything I am writing is emotive. When I travel south by train from Leuchars to Kings Cross, after York I begin to look out for rows of poplar trees and rejoice in the sight of them. I love the smell of privet hedges. At one time John thought that the Roseberry privet hedge was firm enough to walk along the top, and chose Maryan as the lightest to test this. It didn't work and he rushed into the house, shouting, "Quick Mummy, Baby's fallen down into the hedge." She was lifted out unscathed. The sycamore tree proved most useful to children for climbing and for hiding.

A large vegetable garden was made; apple trees, raspberry canes, gooseberry and red and black currant bushes, were planted. We helped to pick the produce and also 'helped' by testing the firmness of jam samples placed in saucers to cool. Jam making and fruit bottling were annual events.

In one of the old farmyard buildings a garage was made – first for my father's motor cycle and then his first and subsequent cars. Our gardener, Tommy Vennard, was a miner and came to help when off shift to earn a bit extra. Later he came to us full time after he was hurt by a fall of coal in the mine, and 'laid off'. He had established himself in one of the outhouses and put up a board on which he had painted TOMMYS OFFICE PRIVATE. When the war came he told my parents he would not go, that he would only run away if the enemy appeared. "Any road I'll just say that the Doctor canny spare me", he added. In the summer of 1918 he was called up despite his handicap. Very soon he was home, having arrived in France on the day of the Armistice, and was delighted to recount his tour of France!

My mother kept some hens and looked after them very efficiently. If any china was broken she just used to say "That will be useful for the hens." She would take the pieces into the yard, smash them up, and put them on a flat stone on which she pounded and ground them up into a gritty powder. This was added to the hens' meal to assist in strengthening the shells of their eggs. Each day a pan of all the scraps, including potato and vegetable peelings, was boiled up on the kitchen range. Into this was mixed meal from the Corn Store, and my mother always made sure it had cooled a bit before she presented the tasty dinner to the hens. How they shoved and clucked and pecked. We had one cockerel who was rather ferocious. One day my mother saw Tommy running at a great speed up the yard and into the washhouse. "Yon booger was after me" he said. "You want to look out for yersel wi' him around."

There was an incident which greatly amused my parents. There was a large attic which could only be accessed by a stepladder put up to the push-up door. None of us ever explored it – it was out of bounds. Periodically my mother decided to clear out the attic, and donned a

159

pinafore and a dust cap. Among other useless items she found a human skull. This had been presented to my father by one of his patients. She took it in its box to Tommy and asked him to a store it somewhere out of reach of the children. Time went by and Tommy in turn decided to have a clear-out. He took the unwanted skull and placed it in the midst of a huge bonfire he had made. When the fire died down he went home. We ran down the garden to investigate. Maryan was about three years old. John had a rake and there was great excitement when he dragged out the skull. We stared at it. "It's a person' s head", John told us. We came to an awful conclusion that Daddy has killed one of his patients. "He might get into trouble," I said. We discussed what steps we should take. We decided that it must be kept secret, but on the other hand we must show our disapproval. We would not speak to him at dinner time. Dinner time came, and soon we were faced with a problem – Daddy did not notice he was being punished. But suddenly Maryan burst into tears, and said, "There's a dead man's head down the garden in the bonfire." John and I confirmed this and the whole family left the table and went down to the kitchen garden. To our astonishment Mummy said, "Tommy's been clearing out", and they both burst out laughing. They explained what had happened, and to our relief and disappointment the drama was punctured.

Tommy's wife Maggie was our washer-woman. She spent all day on Mondays in the washhouse with the poss-tub, the scrubber board, the boiler, the big bowl for the Reckitts Blue and the large wooden mangle. (My mother always provided a hot and especially delicious mid-day dinner on Mondays. She was kind and most thoughtful, and that is one reason why she was so loved.) The clothes were strung out on an enormously long line across the yard. One week the line broke and numerous sheets fell to the muddy ground. As a little boy, John enjoyed drama and on this occasion he danced and shouted and rushed into the kitchen to proclaim the news.

Perhaps what my mother lacked in the early years of her married life was social life and friends, but in time this gap was filled. The midwife who attended my birth was Ethel Brown. She became my godmother and a wonderful, loving, cheerful person she was, beloved by all the family. Over the years she came to stay for many weekends, and she often joined us on holidays. She was promoted in her work and quite soon became Inspector of Midwives for County Durham. She and my parents became good bridge players and enjoyed many happy evenings at this game. The first family friends were the Fergusons. My 'Uncle Fergy' was a most attractive man with a great sense of humour. Aunt Jenny came from a well-born Scottish family. My mother invited the Fergies to the first dinner party she gave as a bride, but from my father's point of view it was not a success. He had put on his best suit and Fergy came in a dinner jacket. After the guests had gone my mother kept telling him it did not matter a bit, but he was mortified. He was usually as cheerful as she was, but sometimes 'went into one of his moods'. She found it best to leave him alone and he was soon smiling again. There was a lot to smile about; my mother always had amusing adventures and stories to tell about the day's events, and her memories. When we were coming home in the car after an outing, I used to wish the journey could go on forever. And I always enjoyed the talk and laughter at the family meal times.

My father liked cats, my mother loved dogs. She bought two female Keeshonds (Dutch Barge dogs), Juno and Chatto, and she bred from them. We adored the successive litters of puppies, and all the fun we had with Juno, Chatto, and a fox terrier called Mick which my father gave me as a present when I was ill. Occasionally this naughty trio would fulfil their dream, escape and go to the woods on the Windleston estate where there was plenty of game to hunt. We called them Ralph Lynn, Tom Walls and Robertson Hare, because when they returned Juno and Chatto breezed in unashamed. Mick brought up the rear, crawling and with his tail down.

My mother, unlike my father, skated and swam and danced well. My father wanted to improve his dancing, and so they engaged a teacher, and invited two couples to come one evening a week. A stock of dance records was acquired for the new wind-up box gramophone: foxtrots, waltzes, valetas, two-steps. Sitting on the stairs (we were meant to be in bed) we heard the strains of all the romantic and sentimental songs of the day. 'Oh Rose Marie I Love You', and so on. There were many dances to come, in the Coundon Badminton Hall, the Kings Hall at Bishop Auckland and elsewhere. Dad was a good tennis player and a red ash court was laid. It needed a lot of attention with a clanking heavy roller. Mummy provided teas in a wooden summerhouse by the court. I don't know why she didn't play. Later a thriving local tennis club was started in a field on the edge of the Windleston woods. The nearby pond was where we learned to skate.

On alternate Saturdays in the football season my parents went to Sunderland to visit my Uncle John and Aunt Ada. The two men (and in later years some of the children) went to see the football match. I don't know when Dad took up golf, but Mum had no interest in the game. My mother enjoyed walking; I think she must have walked for an astounding total of miles on the local country roads and lanes pushing one or other of us in the pram.

When the 1914 war broke out, my father was ready to join up. At his medical examination it was discovered that he had a murmur in his heart. This never affected him in any way. Dr Ferguson went to the war, and returned safely, but it was a sad war for them. Three of Jenny Ferguson's brothers were killed. Only two letters survive of the hundreds my mother at Roseberry wrote to her parents. One tells of an incident during the war. She wrote:

> We have had two air raids in the district. On Monday the gas was lowered at about 9.30, and all the lights had to be put out. We went out into the garden and heard all the noise of engines in the air coming nearer and then going away again for over an hour. It was said to be one of our own Scouts, although there was a Zepp wandering about not far off. On Tuesday Will was out and I heard bombs dropping at Hartlepool before any warning came. I put out the lights and went at once out into the street and got a

man to extinguish a street light at the corner. After that there were a few more explosions and I saw star shells going up, just like fireworks. There were no searchlights at all. It seems Hartlepool got no warning and the lights were on there when the Zepp came. I wish the Germans knew how we take it. Most people aren't a bit afraid, but get rather excited and elated.

In another letter she thanked her father for 'the kippers which arrived last night. They are lovely, so fresh and nicely flavoured. The last we got here were not at all fresh and cost 6d each.' In another letter she wrote of the difficulties of getting food, and that there was 'a riot' in the queue at the Bishop Auckland Co-op. My own and my only memories of the war was that one night my mother came and took me from my cot into their bed, and then later we all went to the window and saw in the distance a zeppelin on fire. My mother made me feel quite secure. It was the same when I was woken by a thunderstorm; she took me to the window to watch and told me it was beautiful to see. My father had a very hard time of it with a large number of visits and long surgeries, especially in the 'flu epidemic after the war. It was a very worrying wartime for my Elgin grandparents. Both Charlie and Wilfred in Canada joined up, Wilfred in the Saskatechewan Regiment. They were both injured in battle. Charlie suffered agony in the truck which took him to the field hospital. He was shot in the back, could not sit down and had to stand for a considerable time leaning over the side of the truck and in great pain. Wilfred's injury was to his face. A German bullet hit the insignia on the uniform of a friend he was talking to, and that dislodged and hit Wilfred in the face. When they found him lying wounded they took him for dead, and put him on a pile of dead soldiers. The next day someone noticed that he was breathing, and his life was saved. He was sent back to England and became one of the first patients of Sir Harold Gilles, the pioneer in plastic surgery. His nose had been shot away, his face badly damaged; extensive skin grafts took place and a new nose was built up. He came to stay at Roseberry while he was recovering.

Now we come to Russell's part in the war. He was eighteen when he joined the Seaforth Highlanders; later he transferred to the Royal Flying Corps. He came to Roseberry to see us twice, once when he was at Catterick Camp and then from Ripon There are two notes of thanks from him; in one he asked 'has Betty's next tooth had come through?' In the summer of 1917 Russell, now a pilot in the Royal Flying Corps, was out in France and due to come home on leave for his twenty-first birthday on 5 July 1917. Word came that he was missing. There was silence until on 23 September 1917 my granny wrote the following letter.

Dearest Mary,

Only a few lines – the worst news came yesterday from The War Office. Our boy is gone. Killed in action on 3rd July. The news was dropped from a German aeroplane into our lines and we are asked not to publish this in the public prints. I mean the means by which we learn the facts. Is this unusual? I do not yet realise that the young promising life is taken and I am left. We had again arranged to go to Kingussie, so intend going tomorrow till Saturday. Father has written to his business people. I am in bed, had muscular rheumatism in shoulder. Very bad pain but now about gone.I think the few days change will do us good. Father is not very strong.

We are so upset. Will you write to Annie, poor girl so far away and all alone.

All my love

Yours, Mother

Later it was possible to find out the place where Russell was buried, and position of the grave. His brothers Gordon and Wilfed went out to see it. In February 1920 my Aunt Ann in New Zealand had the following letter from Keith M.Caldwell, Cambridge, Waikato.

Dear Mrs Moore,

Your letter came last night and I shall be pleased to tell you all I can of Russell. I had no idea that he had any relatives in this part

164

of the world or I should have written before. I cannot give you the exact locality where he fell as neither myself nor any of the other fellows saw the machine crash. But the engagement took place between Crosilles & Marquion – a few miles S.W. of Cambrai, about four miles over the German Lines, as far as I remember. The odds were against us, five against about twenty I think and poor Russell was the first to go down. Shot from underneath by a German Albatross scout painted blue, flown by a pilot by the name of Wolff. This chap was one of their crack shots and before he was killed he brought down over thirty of our machines. Strangely enough he was shot down by a 60 squad pilot a week or two later, so Russell was avenged to some degree. I am quite sure that Russell was killed instantaneously as his Machine went straight out of control and we were unable to watch it for long on account of the fight going on. As you say, his fate was published in a German list sent over to us. But it is strange and disappointing that the Red Cross know nothing about his burial place. The Germans made a habit of burying the occupant or occupants of a machine where the machine fell, and Russell's grave should be between those two towns. There is the chance that the grave was spoiled, when our troops made an advance over that ground later. And I'm afraid that this is likely as I know that the ground about Cambrai. It is just one mass of shell holes etc. I am not sure if the Germans kept any detailed account of the different graves of our fellows and it looks as if they did not. The graves of the R.F.C. were usually reported to our Headquarters by our Infantry units as they advanced over the ground. As far as I know this was about the only source of information except perhaps through the Chaplains appointed especially for that work. After the armistice the Red Cross had started to make a register of all graves in France: the result of this work might reveal something, and is worth while watching. I am sorry that I cannot give you something more definite. Russell had only been with us a short time and was shaping so well that his death was a shock to us all. I know he would have got all sorts of honours if he had the luck that some of us did to keep going a bit longer – but it is great to know that he put in a great show.

Yours sincerely

Keith N. Caldwell.

Russell Adam, RFC, d. 1917

It was a long time before my Grandmother's wish was fulfilled and two of her sons, Gordon and Wilfred went on a mission to France. On 7 May 1957 a letter from the Imperial War Graves Committee was received by Gordon in answer to his letter of enquiry. It stated: 'The Late Lieutenant A.R. Adam, Royal Flying Corps and Seaforth Highlanders, who died on 3rd July, 1917, is buried in Ontario Cemetery, Sains-les-Marquion, France, Plot I. Row E, grave number 2. Sains-les-Marquion is a village in the extreme south of the Department of the Pas-de-Calais on the east side of the Canal du Nord.'

So all that is left of my Uncle Russell are two postcards to my mother; photographs of him; and saddest of all, in an envelope with a band of black for mourning, and inscribed:

Alexander Russell Adam's hair cut
13th April 1897
K.E.R.

In the envelope are thick glossy strands of his pale golden hair tied with silken cord. So this was three months before his second birthday. His life was to be short.

Some time later my mother took me up by train hoping it would cheer my poor Granny and Grandpa. She told me of two incidents which made them laugh. I was left in the sitting room, all dressed up ready to be taken to meet various relatives in a new white dress. When they were ready they came to get me. I had climbed up onto the chair

166

Armistice Day 1918, at Roseberry: Betty, Edith Ferguson and her mother

In the garden at Roseberry: Betty Anderson
with the dog; John with snowball

at Granny's desk, and discovered an inkwell. Picking it up to examine it fell, spilling some of its contents onto my new dress and the rest onto the carpet. The door opened and at once I said "Betty naughty". The other story I was told was that I played with a neighbour's little boy whose name was Johnnie Gentlemen. Next day they found that I was missing and tore out into the street and saw me running. My mother caught me up and picked me up. I protested loudly, saying "Doin' to see Donnie Dentleman."

When the war was over my grandparents used to come down each year and spend their summer holidays with us. We were now able to rent a house at Scarborough (on the North Bay) for a fortnight, and they enjoyed that very much. Our two maids came with us and took us to the sands or to Peaseholm Park, each day and the adults were free to go to the Spa and runs in the car. John (my brother) can recall the sequence of the cars my father had over the many years at Roseberry: a Belsize with an open roof and a dicky; a Rover which they bought at the Motor Show in London, and drove back up the Great North Road; a Citroen, a Talbot, a Lea Francis, a Morris Saloon (Lord Nuffield's inspiration); a Wolseley saloon, a Rover, a Hillman. Having these cars enabled us to go for many picnics, which my granny loved, and to explore the beautiful parts of County Durham. For a time we had 'The Hut' at Bedburn near Hamsterley, and spent happy

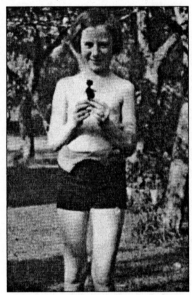

Maryan at Barton Mills

weekends and holidays there. Later, when I was fifteen, they bought Lord Mayors Cottage in Barton Mills, near Mildenhall Suffolk. Our holidays there, in retrospect, were like a wonderful dream. When my mother was in her mid-forties she learned to drive. We called her car the Bucking Bronco; it was a Baby Singer.

Grandpa continued to work until he was about sixty-seven. I think he continued to ship coal and potatoes and distribute them. Then another disaster hit him. His business was destroyed by the coal strike in 1924. It is evident that there was trouble between him and some trustee and he went to litigation and lost the rest of his money. I did not know about this until, when staying at Glassgreen three years ago, I read in recent book a reprint of an article from the *Forres, Elgin and Nairn Gazette* of 16 October 1924. It is headed 'A DEFIANT BANKRUPT' and relates how Mr William Gordon Adam, potato merchant, was examined in bankruptcy by Mr W.S. Urquhart on behalf of Mr T.P.Fraser. In answer to Mr Urquhart Mr Adam said that in his state of affairs he showed assets amounting to £10. That indicates he was not bankrupt.

Mr Adam: "Do you know that I have issued about twenty charges against your witnesses.?"

Mr Urquhart: "I know about your grievances."

Mr Adam: "You have backed these perjurors."

Sheriff: "Will you answer Mr Urquhart's questions?"

So the questions continued. Several times Mr Adam stated that what he was asked was in his in his ledger and cashbook which he had given to them.

As I read the report and knowing my grandfather's honesty and integrity, I felt angry and deeply grieved. He was cross-questioned about whether he had any furniture; his reply was that this was handed over to his wife about twenty four years ago. Then he was asked whether he had an office, and he replied, "I have an office under sufferance."

"Have you any furniture in your office?"

"None. I have the pencil with which I write."

Asked if he had an office or a store in Burghead and where, he made no reply.

Mr Urquhart: "There are ways of dealing with bankrupts who refuse to give information."

Mr Adam: "You can put me in prison if you like."

Sheriff: "I shall not send you to prison unless I have to. You must answer the questions put to you."

Mr Urquhart – "Where did you get the money for the recent litigation you have been carrying on?"

Mr Adam: "I cannnot tell you where. I can show you all that in my cash book. You have got my ledger and cashbook." This led to questioning on where he got the money for a recent holiday costing £12.

Thereupon Mr Urquhart examined him on various entries in the cashbook, repeating his questions. Obviously Mr Adam felt that he was right, the entries were correct, and all this was unfair. He was becoming increasingly tense and angry and frustrated.

Mr Adam "It is a most dishonest thing that a man can do to go into the witness box and commit perjury. It is a disgrace."

Mr Urquhart: "I think your Lordship should seriously warn the witness that steps will be taken against him unless he answers the questions put to him. I suggest that the court be adjourned for a fortnight in order to test some of the answers."

Mr Adam: "I do not wish to come back after a fortnight. I will answer any questions put to me today. I am being insulted."

Sheriff: "Mr Urquhart is doing his duty; it is not a pleasant duty. You must understand that you are in a bankruptcy court. If you do not assist Mr Urquhart in his duty, steps will be taken against you."

Mr Adam: "Mr Urquhart has asked me the same question two or three times. I think you should protect me."

Sheriff: "I will protect you."

Mr Adam: "I will not come back again another day. You can send me to prison or to the gallows if you like."

The examination was adjourned at this stage. What did my grandmother go through at this time? She knew of his honesty and his integrity, of how had he had worked all his life, and of course she supported him. As far as I know he came out of this battle acquitted. I am trying to write about the female line of descent, but such trials as these affected them as much as they did their husbands. My Granny had a grandfather, Peter Merson, who was well–known for standing up for what he thought was right. However he was more litiginous; there are 250 sets of the papers of his lawsuits in the archives.

William Adam was seventy-six when he underwent the above ordeal. He died in on 8 April 1930. Granny continued her summer visits to us, but stayed for a month. Each afternoon she was taken for a drive. When she was a very old lady my parents were staggered by how good her memory was. She would ask at breakfast time where we were to go in the afternoon. On the drive she would ask all sorts of relevent questions. But eventually my mother found that Granny was looking up her last year's notebook! I went up on my own to stay with her when I was in my teens, and something happened which had a great influence on my whole life. I may say it was not a meeting with Johnnie Gentleman! Granny took me to see a nursery school near her house, and I so much enjoyed watching the children (as did she) that, after I had taken a degree at St Andrews University, I went to the Rachel MacMillan Nursery school Training College in Deptford, and that was my line of work.

On the day of my graduation my mother came up from Coundon to St Andrews and my granny came from Elgin. On almost every occasion where my mother was present there was a funny story. When we had celebrated with a lunch party, the invited guests were Connie and Jay (Professor J.A. MacDonald, Botany), we took Granny to Leuchars to get her train home. Although it was July, she had been told St Andrews might be very cold and had brought a fur cape. As the train was pulling out my mother realised that she had the cape over her arm. She sprinted along and reached the right carriage. The window was still open and she flung the fur in, and had just a glimpse of the bizarre sight of the elderly man sitting opposite Granny with the cape over his head.

Granny died on the 19 January 1945. She was never alone. For her last years a faithful maid, whom we called 'Granny's Annie' lived at 24 Hay Street. About 1932 my mother's sister Ann came home back from New Zealand. She rented a flat in London and went to classes in millinery. She then joined some young friends who had a hat shop and made hats – wonderful creations. Granny in Elgin was getting old, and Ann went up to live with her. She started a hat shop at 24 Culbard Street, and it did well. When her mother died Ann bought a pretty cottage at Hopetoun and made a lovely garden specialising in dried flowers. She then married a local man, Leonard Sutherland, and they had a short but happy time together.

CHART J: ABBREVIATED ANDERSON CHART

This Ayrshire family has been traced back to the mid-18th century, but I will start at:

John Anderson, Master Baker, 1840-1923 m.1866 Ann Husband 1846-1919 Kilwinning ch: ten listed, one died in infancy. The following are relevant to the book (I have omitted Janet, Agnes, Ann, Jean, and George d.y.):

1. **James Anderson Master Baker Glasgow 1867-1919 m. Jessie Galbraith ch:**
    (1) Bessie
    (2) John b.1902
    (3) Annie Anderson b.1905 m. John McConnell ch:
        1. Jan McConell b.1935 2. Allan McConnell b.1938 m. Lesley McKay ch:
    David McConnell m. Karen Aitken ch:
        (1) David McConnell b.1997
        (2) Stewart McConnell b.2002

2. **John Anderson MB ChB 1869-1954, Sunderland m. Ada Giles ch:**
    (1) Gavin John Anderson MA Cantab. 1906-19 m. Grace Ward ch:
        1. Ruth Anderson b 1937 m. Patrick Riggall
        2. Susan Anderson b.1951 m. Peter Stewart ch:
            (1) Joseph Stewart b.1982
            (2) Robin Stewart b.1984
        3. Philip Anderson b.1951

(2) Henry Dale Anderson MB ChB 1907-1999 m. Margery
Moor 1910-1989 ch:
   1. Jenifer Anderson b.1938 m. Robert Campbell 1960 ch:
      (1) Heather Campbell b.1961
      (2) Andrew Campbell b. 1963 m. Alison Lowery ch:
          Megan b.1989
      (3) William Campbell b.1967

   2. Eleanor Anderson b.1947 m. Hugh Holme ch:
      (1) Ralph Holme b.1974 m. Sarah Johnstone ch:
          Oliver George Holme b.2003
      (2) Matthew Holme b.1976 m. Catherine Harris ch:
          Esme Eleanor Holme b.2004
      (3) Philip Holme b.1978

(3) Marjorie Anderson 1913-1983 unm.

3. Margaret (Meg) Anderson b.1874 m. Dr John Welsh ch:
   Dr Thomas Welsh unm.

7. Robert Anderson b.1876 m. Margaret McDonald emigrated to
Boston ch:
   (1) Edmund Anderson
   (2) Mabelle Anderson m. Henry Natelson (desc)
   (3) Margaret Anderson m. John Chandler

10. William Greig Anderson b.1886 m. Mary Gordon Adam
(see Chart K, Chapter 12)

CHAPTER 12

FOUR GENERATIONS

A fter the wonderful years at St Andrews University I did the graduates' course at the Rachel McMillan College in Deptford, and qualified as a Nursery School and kindergarten teacher. Just before my twenty-first birthday I became engaged to Rex Willsher, a friend of my Sunderland Anderson cousins. We were married at Barton Mills. The service was conducted by the Revd. Mr Dams, with whom I had an altercation a few days before the wedding. Rex and I could not agree on one thing; I wanted the revised service because I did not want to take the vow to obey. We asked to discuss the matter with the Rector. I explained that I did not believe that a wife had to

Wedding of Betty Anderson and Rex Willsher at Barton Mills

Four Generations: Betty (centre) with her mother, her Granny Keturah and her baby Penny

obey her husband simply because he was a man. I was amazed when Mr Dams upheld Rex's point of view about the duties of a woman. There was nothing to be done; some of the guests had already left for the wedding. It may be that I have inherited some genes from my grandfather William Adam and my great-grandfather Peter Merson. I hope so.

We had bought a small semi-detached house in Blackheath. Rex was the manager of an animal feeding stuffs mill in Bermondsey, and my job was to be the first nursery school teacher in a Day Nursery which was one of a handsome row of houses at Wapping Pierhead, and looked onto the Thames. I had to work my way in against the resistance of the head nurse. It was like swimming upstream against a strong current, but with the help of a kind and wise matron I reached dry land. I was sad when I had to leave three months before our first child was born. Her name was Anne Penelope; I think I was ignorant of the old family naming customs. But Penelope was the right name for her; one of her characteristics is loyalty and perseverance. However she has always been known as Penny. She arrived promptly on Easter Sunday, 2 April 1937. I went into the nursing home at Lewisham at eight o'clock. It was owned by two sisters – one the Matron, one the Sister! They were so good and kind to me. Matron said to me later that day, "You are our best ever patient. A beautiful baby and we had our breakfast in peace and now we can have our Easter Sunday dinner uninterrupted." My mother had come to stay three days before, and both she and Rex were delighted when they saw Penny for the first time. She looked perfect. There was a letter from my mother in the post next morning.

Dearest Betty,

I am sorry I won't be able to see as much of you and the lovely baby as I would like, but I shall have to go back on Tuesday. I'll come at four o'clock tomorrow. I wish I could stay. Rex is going about with a continuous smile; he can't get over the fact that Miss Willsher is such a personality already. She is so beautiful and looks so self-possessed. I have just been on the phone to Roseberry and everyone is so pleased.

Much love from Mummy

I read this with pleasure. It was wonderful, it was amazing. The regime then was à la Truby King and I stayed at the nursing home for almost three whole weeks! By the time I took Penny home she was 'trained'. I fed her every four hours, and she slept all night. After each feed she was weighed to see exactly how much she had taken, and this soon established the length of time of feeding. My mother came to stay again when Penny and I were home. I remember how keen she was to push the pram and how pleased we both were. Years later I read a book by Laurie Lee, *The Firstborn*, and was very struck with the following description of his own baby. He wrote, 'She fills the cottage with her obsessive purpose. The rhythmic tides of her feeding and sleeping spaciously measure the days and nights. Her frail self-absorption is a commanding presence, her helplessness as strong as a rock, so that I find myself listening to her silences as though some great engine was purring upstairs.'

I managed to take Penny up to Coundon while my granny was

staying there, and we went to Bishop Auckland to the photographer's so that a four generation photo might be taken. Then we returned to Blackheath. The peace and contentment of our lives did not last for long. The first barrage balloons were being hoisted over London like grotesque grey jumbos. The Ministers were holding frantic meetings and last minute attempts to avoid war. Towards the end of August we went to Suffolk for our summer holiday, a family holiday at Barton Mills with my parents, my sister Maryan and brother John. We played tennis, we swam at the pool at the end of Dr Fleming's garden (this was the Alexander Fleming who discovered penicillin, and who had a holiday house at Barton Mills). We had picnics and we went for walks over Cherry Hill. And we listened to the news anxiously. When it seemed that war was inevitable my family went north. Maryan was due to start at St Andrews as a medical student in October. Rex had already returned to London, having been summoned to a Civil Defence meeting in the Rotherhithe area. I said goodbye to my family and they took my luggage over to Worlington House (about a mile away). Uncle John and Aunt Ada had promised to have Penny and myself. Next morning I cleared up the cottage and after lunch set out, pushing Penny in the pram. We called at the Village Hall, and I was worried when I was told that the babies' gas masks had not yet arrived. I walked along the familiar road, past the church along by the flat meadows, by Parker's Dairy. It seemed it must surely be a nightmare.

At Worlington House there was a scene of great activity. My aunt and uncle and my cousin Margery were hard at work white-washing the porches, conservatory and greenhouses. It was explained to me that this was in case the glass gleamed in the moonlight and the Germans thought it was a factory. It was a hot day and eventually we gave up.

In the night Margery and I were woken up by the grim wailing of an Air Raid warning. She helped me carry Penny in her Moses Basket down the back stairs to the sitting room. All I could think of was that there was no gas mask for Penny. Marjorie and I went up to waken her parents. We knocked and knocked. Eventually the door opened. "ALL RIGHT", Uncle John said crossly, "ALL RIGHT", and reluctantly they came down. He lit the fire and made tea. And Penny slept peacefully. After a time my uncle said, "We've given them enough time. We will all go back to bed now." It was some time before the All Clear sounded.

Next morning we went back to the white-washing and almost missed the broadcast by Mr Chamberlain announcing that we were at war. That evening Aunt Ada (who was a nurse) told me that she thought it might be difficult to have us to stay there as she had plans to have a clinic in the house which would be used by all local evacuees. My solution came immediately. Rex rang me to say that our friends Doreen and Gilbert Cook, who had just moved to a new house in Kent, had invited us to stay there. Gilbert was in a Government department and was often away for brief spells. Doreen was expecting their first baby. So we packed up once again, Rex came, and we settled in at Orpington. I remember an amusing incident. One day Gilbert was up a tree picking apples, and a man who was walking past, thinking Gilbert was the gardener, hailed him. "My man", he said, "Go in and tell your mistress that the child has flung itself out of its perambulator and is suspended upside down by its bridle." "Aye aye, sir", said Gilbert and touched his cap. Penny appeared quite unperturbed and was examining the spokes of the wheels with interest. Many years later her interests lay in physics and chemistry.

John Cook was born in February and Penny took a great interest in him. The war news was threatening, and one Sunday when we had just started our mid-day dinner, what was to be called The Battle of Britain began with the increasingly loud roar of low planes overhead. Gilbert said, "Don't let them spoil a good meal. Take your plates to the shelter." This was a part of the sitting room just under the staircase. The noise increased and the planes seemed to almost touching the roof. Penny began to cry, and Doreen gave her a piece of chocolate – her first taste ever. A blissful expression came over her face. After the

All Clear Gilbert went out to see what had happened and came back looking grave. The Air Raid Wardens had taken shelter in a ditch nearby and he was told that one plane had just missed the roof of our house. They had seen some of our fighters shot down. Next day we fled, Penny, Rex and myself to Bedfordshire to his parents and the Cooks to stay with Gilbert's parents.

I was expecting another baby and three months before the birth Penny and I went up to stay at Roseberry. Penny was a joy to everyone. She used to sit on my father's knee when he was smoking a pipe, and give it a tap so that some ash spilled onto his jacket. Then she would say reprovingly "Naughty Poppa spilled, Peepy get brush." She brushed off the ash in a business like way, and then said "'gen please".

She called herself "Peepy", but one day she and I were out for a walk – without the pram. Some boys were playing in a tent on a green, and she ran up and put her head in the flap. "Hello boys", she said. They laughed. "What's your name?" they asked her. She beamed and replied "My name is Pellepoly Busybody Wookey Willsher", and they shouted with laughter. She was very reluctant to continue our walk.

Our second daughter, Susan, was born in a Nursing Home at Barnard Castle. I remember the awful nights when the noise of aeroplane engines came down the chimney and seemed to fill the room. We stayed for a week or so; it was good to be back home and see Penny so delighted with her new sister. She was assiduous in helping me. One Sunday morning the Leasingthorne Colliery Band arrived just after we had bathed the baby and I was feeding her. Penny had decided to empty the bath by scooping up water in the potty, and carrying it to a hand basin at the end of the passage. She was arrested by the music and went to the front door. Some of the younger players began to laugh and, disconcerted, Penny flung the contents of the potty onto the lawn, waved and ran inside. There was a pause in the recital while the bandmaster called the men and boys to attention.

We had one bad experience at Coundon. The dining-room had been turned into a bedroom for myself and the little girls. We were sound asleep one night when the siren went; almost immediately bombs exploded nearby. There was a crash of glass; one of the windows had been blown in. I jumped out of bed and, confused, was unsure whether to pick up the baby or Penny. Maryan was there at once and we went through the kitchen and through the wash-house into the shelter. Maryan made tea and my mother went to the spare room to find Dr Benson, a small lady who was the current medical assistant. She had been blown out of bed and was stunned but not hurt. It wasn't long before there was a banging on the back door and a voice shouted "Come out doctor, the wounded's being brought to the surgery, and the wardens think there's mebbe an unexploded bomb down your garden." "Don't go down to see Daddy", I said urgently. It turned out that a plane had jettisoned a string of bombs and the first of these had blasted away the front of one of the miners' houses in the nearest row of the block by the road. Astonishingly the couple who had been asleep in a double bed were jettisoned into the air and, still in the bed, landed unhurt in the back lane. One or two others had minor injuries. The rest of the bombs had fallen in the field in front of Roseberry. Maryan and I went out at dawn to view the horrifying scene, the great row of craters with the brown earth around each one. The half house displayed the grimness of war. The war news was bad. The allies were suffering heavy shipping losses Later Churchill said "the only thing that really frightened me during the war was the U-boat peril."

Our major cities were being pounded by bombing. Then the news came that Hitler was using incendiary bombs. At Roseberry, Penny and the baby Susan played a major part of our own lives. Penny made friends with the gardener Mr Embleton who had replaced Tommy Vennard. She used to say "Going to see Embly", trot off down the garden, and have long conversations. He said of her, "By she's a canny one, she's a little hinny". I had now been at home for three months and when my parents offered us the use of the cottage at Barton Mills we accepted it eagerly. So once again I packed up. The car was loaded with our cases and we were leaving for the train at Darlington. Penny went off to find Embly to say goodbye. When she returned she was holding a little blue flower he had given her. "It's called a forget-a-don't" she told us.

Barton Mills was an ideal place to spend the rest of the war. We made many good friends, and when Susan was two I started a little nursery school. Rex was keen to help the war effort by keeping some animals. Somehow hens and duck and geese turkeys and a donkey called Jacob took up residence in the very large garden. On the advice of a helpful elderly neighbour I acquired a sixteen year-old girl, Hazel, who was a wonderful aide. School was a picnic, the farm a battle. Hens got egg bound; the turkeys roosted in trees by the road and terrified passers-by. The ducks refused to go into their shed at night. The goats managed to cross the ditches and browse in the vegetable garden of the Bull Inn, which did little for my reputation. So they had to be tethered. In protest they walked in circles until their heads were lowered and they were gasping .The donkey refused to walk across the main road at the Bull Inn, and this caused a hold up of a convoy of army trucks. The drivers were all American Africans; the one in the first truck put his head out of the window and shouted, "Well sink ma soul if it ain't an ass." He got down and helped me with the recalcitrant beast.

We had a load of furniture brought down from Blackheath. Our house had been bombed, but this had survived. Rex made the end part of the garage into a place for the geese at night, and the furniture filled up the rest of the space. But one morning to my horror I found that the geese had made a gap in the netting and had been roosting in the more comfortable chairs. Hazel gallantly helped me to clear up the disgusting mess.

There was a credit side to this. Rex greatly enjoyed the respite from the war in Rotherhithe and loved the farmyard. Later he became a farm manager. The animals, especially the donkey, gave great pleasure to Penny and Susan and the nursery children. I was one of a group of mothers who set up a kindergarten near Mildenhall. Penny was five and began 'Big School' with confidence. She always looked forward to being grown up; this seemed to her a big step towards that goal. It was all very successful.

After a time I became a landlady. One day a young Army officer came to the door. He was stationed in the are and his wife and new baby were in County Durham. He was searching for some rooms so that they could be together. So before long Mary and John Bradley and their little son settled into two rooms, and shared the bathroom and kitchen with us. It was a great success; they stayed for a year when they had to go to a new posting. I was a bit worried that Penny was spending quite a lot of time after breakfast with Mary and the baby. I went in to see if she was being a nuisance, and found her sitting in an armchair with the baby on her knee. Mary came back with water for the baby's bath and I asked her if she was sure it was all right. "It certainly is", she told me. "In fact I couldn't do without Penny's help. She knows what to do and I don't."

During the 1939–1945 War my father increased the number of hours he spent training ambulance workers and in 1943 he was awarded the Ambulance Workers' V.C. My mother trained with the Red Cross and, as Commandant, went on to train local girls. I remember how pleased she was when two or three of them went in for full time nursing. We were all very proud when she went to London at a time when the bombing was bad, to do a week's relief work in the air raid shelters. She was at my brother John's graduation at St Andrews in 1945 and my sister Mayan's at St Andrews in 1947. They were both medicals. Her greatest delight for many years was her grandchildren, my daughters Penny and Susan who went regularly to stay at Roseberry.

CHART K: ABBREVIATED CHART OF DR WILLIAM ANDERSON AND MARY ADAM

William Grieg Anderson MB ChB 1886-1963 m. 1913 Mary Gordon Adam 1883-1955 ch:
1. **Elizabeth Cameron Anderson MA MBE b.1915** m.28.8.1937 Rex Willsher 1911-1998 ch:
    (1) **Anne Penelope Willsher MA** Oxon. b 2.4.1939 m.2.7.1962 John Walker MA Oxon. b.11.6.1937 ch:
       1. Elizabeth Janet Walker LLB b.14.8.1965 m.31.12.2001 Andrew Kelly LLB ch: Bethan Rose b.2.11.2002; Niame Rosanne 28.7.2004
       2. David Robert John Walker b.2.4.1967 partner Kumi ch: Aya b.31.7.2004

    (2) **Susan Jane Willsher MA** Oxon. b.6.3.1941 m. 24.4.1963 Neville John Davidson Kelly MA Oxon. b.28.2.1941 ch:
       1. Kirsteen Mary Davidson Kelly MA Mus.Hons 1 (Edinburgh) b.21.9.1967 m. Bertrand Fritsch BSc Hons C.Eng. b.29.11.1966 ch:
          (1) Eloise Fritsch b.16.8.2000
          (2) Zhana Fritsch b.14.11.2003
       2. Sally Keturah Davison Kelly MA Hons 1 (Edinburgh) b.15.11.1970 m. Luke Francis MA ch:
          (1) Josie Francis b.18.7.2000
          (2) Lola Francis b.7.5.2001

2. **John Russell Anderson** MB ChB MD CBE b.31.5.1918, Professor Pathology Glasgow University m. 18.10.1956 Audrey Margaret Shaw Wilson MBChB b.30.12.1928 ch:
    (1) **Kenneth William Anderson** BVMS b.5.9.1957 m.1.9.1982 Anthea Mills Green b.30.9.1954 ch:

1. Thomas Russell Anderson b.9.4.1985
2. Amy Elizabeth Anderson b.9.5.1986
(2) **Alan Russell Anderson** MSc Forestry Science b.26.4.1959
m.26.6.1984 Julie Evelyn Muir b.3.7.1962 ch:
1. Finlay Anderson b.3.18.1990
2. Murdo Anderson b.30.9.1993
(3) **Susan Mary Anderson** b.22.1.1961 d.13.2.1985
(4) **Lois Elizabeth Anderson** b.28.5.1966 partner Robert Ings
b.1967 ch:
1. Katherine Keturah Ings b.1991
2. Rowan Mary Ings b.1993
3. Franklin John Ings b.1996

3. **Maryan Gordon Anderson** MB ChB b.11.2.1923 m.12.4.1964
John Hardcastle Huntridge CBE b.15.5.1920 ch:
Amanda Mary Huntridge b.18.3.1964 partner Thomas
William Dixon ch:
1. Jack Huntridge Dixon b. 20.10.1998
2. CharlesThomas Huntridge Dixon b.25.6.2000
3. Arthur John and Willa Huntridge Dixon
b.26.7.2004

CHAPTER 13

CHILDREN, GRANDCHILDREN, GREAT-GRANDCHILDREN

The Christmas of 1949 was memorable. The whole family was together at Roseberry. Penny was ten years old and Susan was eight. A few days after Christmas my brother John drove me up to St Andrews, Fife, to our new home. This was a three-storey stone house on the Lade Braes. Our furniture arrived next day, and we got everything into place. The large upstairs drawing room was to be the nursery school, and – to my relief – the new tables and chairs and boxes of equipment came right on time. I had advertised in the *St Andrews Citizen* and had a full list to start the new term. John then went back to Glasgow to the University where he was now senior lecturer in Pathology. All was ready when my mother and the girls arrived. I was at St Andrews station to meet them.

Just along the lane were the playing fields, the swing park, the Kinnessburn with ducks all the way up to the millpond. Before my mother went home we explored St Andrews; she loved it, especially the Botanic Gardens at the Bute. I took Penny and Susan to see their new school, St Katharines, to meet the Headmistress, Miss Ludgate, and to get their new school uniform. The woollen hats were always known as 'jelly bags', the blouses and skirts and coats were beige. The girls settled in smoothly and happily and soon made friends. And so did I. We acquired a cat called Philip. At weekends we explored on our bykes. A favourite picnic place was along the east sands, past the Kinkell Braes and the Maiden Rock and before the Rock and Spindle – a little bay with golden sand and a mysterious little cave in the cliff above.

Coronation Day 1953 is still vivid in my mind. There was an assembly of children at the Madras College for a fancy-dress parade.

After the prizes were awarded, the long procession made its way to Cockshaugh Park. There were games and refreshments, but it was a day of bitterly cold wind, so before long we went home and had hot baths. The parents of one of my nursery school children had invited us to their house, and here we saw our first programme on television. It was very exciting – almost as if we were at the solemn and moving ceremony of the coronation of our Queen. It was a long time before we had a television, and I had no car until 1963.

Both Penny and Susan went as Day Girls from St Katharines to St Leonards School. They came home on their bicycles at lunchtime. I think of them rushing in, rosy cheeked and full of the news of the day. "What's for lunch?" they would cry, and one day when I said "Shepherd's Pie", they both said "SUPER".

This is Penny's reply to my request to recall some of her memories of living in St Andrews:

> The discipline and orderliness of the school suited me well, and certain teachers influenced me greatly. Apart from cricket, I enjoyed playing games every day, although in the winter the games fields were very exposed, and in those days we didn't wear track suits. Sometimes in the summer we used to go swimming at the West Sands or in the Step Rock Pool; the seawater was usually icy cold. At school our swimming lessons were in a tidal rock pool with no changing facilities. It was compulsory to go to classical concerts in school and, although I didn't appreciate it at the time, I realised later that the professional performers were often top level.
>
> Susan and I both worked very hard and didn't have much spare time, but we played together and with our friends at weekends. All three of us enjoyed walks along the east sands and the cliffs, and cycle rides in the country. I particularly remember one breakfast picnic in a disused quarry where the honeysuckle was in flower. [*This was at Newton of Nydie, out past Strathkinness High Road. In later years we had evening barbecues there. One time I was there and was amazed when a deer ran by.*]
>
> In the winter we learnt to skate on the Pipeland Bowling Green pond. I recall the smell of the acetylene lamps which were lit after

dark so that we could go on skating. Each year we were delighted by the Kate Kennedy procession as it went through the town.

Our Uncle John sometimes took us on exciting outings. Once, just after the news of the successful ascent of Hilary and Tensing to the summit of Mount Everest, Uncle John arrived in a Rolls Royce! He was waiting for a new car, and had hired this splendid gleaming spacious vehicle. (It was one of two which were given to a butler by his employers when he retired from service with them; he set up a business as a taxi driver and occasionally hired out one of his cars.) We had a great day out; we drove up to the Sma' Glen five miles north of Crieff, and we picnicked by the River Almond. Then Uncle John, Susan and I climbed the hill, stopping from time to time to wave and shout to Mummy below, "CAMP ONE, CAMP TWO, CAMP THREE" – . [*This was the first time the girls had seen the hills, had been so far north. My memory of this outing was that on the way north I turned round to see Penny sitting in the spacious back of the car, absorbed in her physics homework. I asked her to look at the view. She glanced round and turned back to her book. I told her that physics were not important enough to work at on an outing. Her reply wass: "They certainly are. Do you know that the bridge we have just passed over could never have been built if it was not for physics?" I realised then how narrow my education had been.*]

Another memorable half term break was when Uncle John took the three of us up to Loch Awe. We stayed at the fishing hotel at Port Sonnachan. John hired a boat and had brought an outboard motor. We did some fishing, then we went to one of the little islands and had a walk there. There was a young boy herding a flock of sheep. On the way back the engine broke down so we rowed the boat back, which was fun. (We had learned to row at Craigtoun Park.) Another time we went to Pitlochry by train, stayed in a B&B and explored the countryside.

There are other disjointed memories. Next door but one lived the three Miss Robertsons. They kept watch lest we rode our bikes down John Street, or lest our cat Philip had not been taken in and put to bed. Once a year they had a great spring-cleaning. Their rugs and carpets were hung on the clothes-line and beaten with cane rackets. One day when we came back from school their six fur coats were on the line! [*This was the time when Penny came rushing in and cried "Maman, les Trois Ours sont denudés."*]

At one time we took in a student to board with us. She turned out to be a very nervous person. One summer night when we were all asleep, there were fearful screams from her room. We rushed down to her aid. She was completely hidden under the blankets and shouting hysterically that a vampire had come in through the window, landed on her bed, and when she put her hand out to put on the light, had sucked blood from her arm. When Mummy put the light on, she saw a bird on the bed, caught it, and took it down to the garden. We made tea and comforted the poor student.

I also remember Mummy having friends to meals and how lively and jolly they were. One night after a party she was washing up. She had put all the crystal glasses on a tray and as she was taking them to a cupboard she slipped. There was the most tremendous crash. Susan and I jumped out of our beds and ran down. She was sitting in the middle of a heap of broken glass. Every single glass was broken. When she saw our dismay, she got up and said, "Don't worry, we will get new cheap ones from Woolworths, and then we need never worry in case they get broken."

The worst thing that happened was an incident in the night. Susan had two lovely white rabbits. They lived in a roomy hutch in a little porch built off the dining room. Susan gave them freedom in the garden, and in winter she used to bring them into the dining-room in the evening. They were a great joy to her. One morning she was up early and went down to feed them. The hutch was empty; its wire door was damaged. Susan went into the garden and saw the mangled blood-covered bodies of her pets. We found that a dog had got in and done this. The police traced the owner and found the dog was the culprit of other misdemeanours and it had to be put down. It was a terrible thing for Susan.

I will now take over from Penny. Looking back I find those years have telescoped in my mind, and seem amazingly distant. I remember going to St Leonards to watch hockey and lacrosse matches, and to a succession of annual Sports Days. In the summer the great event was the garden party. The girls wore white dresses and white gloves, and handed round cups of tea and plates of sandwiches and cakes. And of course the proud parents were all dressed up. The girls gave wonderful dance displays and gym displays. The sun shone, just as in my memories it always did for events at St Andrews.

My parents were delighted with their granddaughters and so pleased when I sent copies of their school reports. The three of us spent part of each holiday at Roseberry. But this family happiness was cut short. In the autumn of 1954 my mother was ill, and the diagnosis was that she had a rare form of cancer called myelotesis. She was very brave, bore the attacks of severe pain, and was typically cheerful and optimistic. On Christmas Day 1954 we were all with her. John was back from a year of medical research in USA. Daddy and John carried Mummy downstairs and she was seated at the head of the table. She was so cheerful. She said afterwards it was the best Christmas Day ever. She died on 2 January 1955. As in the life of her mother, she was never alone, always cared for and loved. Maryan had come home and looked after her for several weeks. My father tackled his future with courage, and took over the task of writing me a letter every week. Instead of retiring, as they had planned, he stayed on in the practice for some time. He had a very good housekeeper, and eventually bought a house in Scarborough; we all had many happy holidays there. On 9 December 1963 my father died at home after a short illness. Maryan was with him and had nursed him. He had been a good and generous father to us and a good grandfather to our children. I have not said much about the Anderson side of the family. This is not because they did not matter; of course they did, but it is not in my remit.

On 18 October 1956 we all met in Glasgow for a very special event, the wedding of my brother John at Milngavie. The beginning of that story was that John had been climbing and met a friend up in the hills. This friend introduced him to his companions and said, "But you will know Audrey – she attended your pathology lectures as a student." They shook hands, talked for a bit and then John went on his way. When he got back he went to the University and spent quite some time going through the class lists. At last he settled on Audrey Wilson of Milngavie as being the one. He invited her out – and she *was* the right one. When John wrote a few lines for me about his war years and his work in Glasgow, he said that living in digs and working tremendously hard, a long day and part of the night, was arduous. He added 'and then I met Audrey and after that everything was all right'. For a long time they lived in a house called Barnellan in the country parish of Baldernock. Four children were born, Kenneth, Russell, Susan and Lois. It was a family who loved the countryside of Scotland, who walked, climbed, skied, rode, sailed, camped and caravanned. Perhaps I have used the wrong tense; they and their children still enjoy such things. John and Audrey and family moved to Liverpool when John accepted the chair of Pathology there, but returned when he was offered the chair at Glasgow University. I think John inherited one of our grandfather Adam's traits: that of working very hard. He is still indefatigable. In the days when he had to drive the children to their Glasgow schools each morning, he was up at five to work on new editions of Muir's *Pathology*. Now as his voluntary work he grows trees to plant put on public places, combatting mice, moles, squirrels, and root diseases and droughts. Audrey is a great gardener, charity worker and cook.

My sister Maryan was married to John Huntridge of Cambridge on 12 April 1963 in the Savoy Chapel at 10 a.m. I was staying with Susan at Epsom and we met them afterwards and had coffee at the Savoy. Then they rushed off to have lunch with John's parents. Maryan continued to work full time in her own medical practice in Cambridge. When she retired she was described as 'the doyenne of general practitioners'. She and John have one daughter, Amanda Mary, who lives in Norfolk and now has two sons. Many of us in the family are keen gardeners; it was Amanada who qualified as a landscape gardener. Every summer when I am south staying with Penny we meet for a family picnic half way between the two homes. The lunch is splendid; my sister is a notable cook and hostess. It is good to see Amanda and her two boys who brim with life and enthusiasm. The last picnic was in Bedfordshire at the Shuttleworth aeroplane museum; John Huntridge had been managing director of Marshalls at Cambridge, so the exhibits were of great interest to him and his grandsons.

So I return to St Andrews and Penny and Susan. Penny was head of Day Girls' House, and later Susan was head. First Penny, and then Susan, won bursaries for Somerville College Oxford. Penny read chemistry, and Susan P.P.E., as she wished to become a social worker. Penny writes, 'It was a new world and a new social life.' I looked forward to her weekly letters. One week she wrote to tell me that she had met a law student called John Walker from Yorkshire at the Presbyterian Church. I knew about this church. The Minister, John Thornton, had been at Martyrs' Church in St Andrews, and I had been at his wedding to Patricia Greenwood, who was on the staff of St Leonards. They invited first Penny and then Susan to their home in Oxford. Penny and John Walker got engaged, and it has turned out very well. Then Susan wrote and told me that she had made a new friend at the same church, John Davidson Kelly from Edinburgh, up at Exeter College and studying history. All four got 2/1 Honours degrees. Penny and John were married near Leeds on 21 July 1962, and Susan and John at Greyfriars' Church Edinburgh in April 1964. John is related through his mother to the Macleods, chiefs of Dunvegan Castle, and Dame Flora invited John and Susan to spend part of their honeymoon there. Susan told me with a twinkle in her eyes that it was a new experience to be woken by the butler at the bedside with a tray of tea. Their first home was in Epsom where John had a post as master at Epsom College. Not long after they were married, Susan and John bought a house on Skye and spent the school holidays there. This was my introduction to many happy holidays on that wonderful island.

After Penny and John's wedding and their honeymoon in St Andrews, they lived in a rented flat in Leeds, where John was with a firm of solicitors doing his articles. Penny had a job as a scientific information

Wedding of Penny Willsher and John Walker, July 1962

Wedding of Susan Willsher and John Davidson Kelly, April 1963

officer with Coal Tar Research. The next year they bought a small terraced house at Leeds. Their first child, my first grandchild, was born in hospital on 14 August 1965. I had promised to be there and had rather a rush to get away from my work. Driving south in my Morris Mini, I was disconcerted when I was overtaken by a police car and told to pull in. They had noticed that my car licence was not the right colour. I had forgotten to renew it. I was told that I should go to a post office nearby and get it renewed. I told them why I was in a hurry. I was pleased when one of them, smiling, said, "You don't look old enough to be a granny." They were very kind and told me to continue, and then not to use the car until I could get the licence renewed.

The baby was a little girl. Penny and the baby were in hospital for three days. They were driven home in an ambulance; I was looking for them and rushed out. The ambulance driver lifted Janet from her Moses basket, carried her to me, and put her in my arms. "She's all yours, Grandma", he said. I was quite overcome. I had the strangest feeling that this was Penny as a baby, and she really was mine. Her name was Elizabeth Janet. Elizabeth was my name, my granny's second name and *her* Granny Merson's name. When Janet grew up and went to university she became Elizabeth, and since then she has always been known as Liz. Her little brother, David Robert John, was born at home on 2 April (his mother's birthday) 1967. Again I was there. Just after his birth he suffered the trauma of having the midwife throw a basin of cold water over him. The following night he yelled for several hours. Obviously he had very good lungs. John and I paced the downstairs in turn, carrying and rocking him. I remember that one time when I went to take over, John looked at me and said "Whatever are you meant to do with them?" David thrived, and Janet was a kind, gentle and helpful sister.

When John qualified as a solicitor he chose High Wycombe, Buckinghamshire, as the area where he would like to work: a country area with some industry. He was accepted by a good family firm Allan Janes & Co., and later became one of the partners, and then the senior partner. For a few years the Walkers lived at Downley near High Wycombe, and then moved to a fine, but run-down, house with a big garden at Gerrards Cross. There the children grew up, and Penny and John gradually renovated the house and are still there enjoying it, as well as the lovely garden they have made, and the countryside. Penny soon got a part-time job nearby in Chalfont St Peter as a scientific information officer with the International Bee Research Association, and it suited her well. But in 1986 the Association moved to Cardiff. Penny continued to work with the retired director, Dr Eva Crane, and to do free-lance work from home.

Penny writes: 'Janet was conscientious, determined and sociable. In her teens she excelled at sports and developed a bubbly personality with a great sense of humour and fun. And she has always been a very loyal person. She went to Cardiff University where she got a law degree, and then qualified as a solicitor. In her 'gap' year she worked

Descendants of Keturah Russell wearing a dress which she wore aged about 7: left, Susan Willsher; above Susan's daughter Sally Keturah (dress hem shortened); right, Amanda Huntridge

Kirsteen and Sally Davidson Kelly

for six months in Australia and travelled for the rest of the year. She completed her training with a large London law firm and then specialised in sports law. She moved to Bristol, renewing a friendship with another solicitor, an ex-university friend, Andrew Kelly. On New Year's Eve 2001, they were married in the hall of Clearwell Castle in the Forest of Dean. We were all there and stayed for the night. For me the most moving moment was when Liz walked up to the altar to the tune 'It had to be you, wonderful you'. Everything had turned out all right – more than all right – the song said it all. The musicians of the family entertained us before and after the ceremony. The pièce de resistance was an arrangement (by John Davidson Kelly) of *Highland Cathedral* for keyboard (Kirsteen Davidson Kelly), bagpipes (John D.K.), drums (David Walker) and trumpet (John Walker).

Something must be said about David who is important to all of us. Penny writes: 'As often happens with siblings, David had different attributes from his sister. He was not very happy at school but blossomed in other ways: he was a comic and very imaginative – and also musical. From an early age he took risks; for example at a school party when he was 5, he was the first to volunteer for a ride on the shoulders of a uni-cyclist. As an adult, he reads a lot and writes fluently. When he was 25 he went to live in Hong Kong and pursued his music there, and he also plays in Thailand and mainland China. He lives on a small peaceful island. He comes back to visit everyone in the UK at intervals, and between visits we keep in touch by e- mail, a great modern boon.'

Susan and John Davidson Kelly lived at Epsom for sixteen years.

Penny and John Walker's son David and daughter Janet (or Liz)

Wedding of Liz Walker and Andrew Kelly, New Year's Eve, 2001

Susan had qualified as a social worker and had her first post working with handicapped people, residents at an Epsom home. Later she specialised in Child Care. A very caring and conscientious person, her work was of great importance to her. Besides teaching, John was head of Day Boys' House, he coached rugger teams, he was a centre of social life, and he became well known as a piper. One day he told Susan that he had to play at weddings on the next three Saturdays. She said, "Isn't there anyone else in the south of England who plays the pipes?' Susan and John's first baby was a girl, Kirsteen Mary. Kirsteen was a radiant little girl with a strong imagination. When she was about a year old, and could say a few single words, they were doing the long journey to Skye by night. The lights in Perth always held them up, and when the car stopped a little voice from the back of the car said "What's up now?", astonishing her parents. A second girl was born when Kirsteen was three, and to my delight was baptised Sally Keturah. Their early years were spent in a large house, which had been flatted for school staff. The staff who lived here became great friends and the small group of young children had wonderful times playing in the big garden.

Susan and John told stories and read many books to the little girls. Among Kirsteen's favourites were Alison Uttley's *Little Grey Rabbit* books, and I was able to send her soft toys of some of the characters. I was fortunate enough to stay in Skye with them each summer, and I recall going for a walk with Kirsteen to gather bog cotton 'to make stuffing for a pillow for Little Grey Rabbit'. Kirsteen and Sal have always been close, and used to play marvellous games together, Kirsteen usually taking the leading role: hairdressers, air hostesses, and a radio announcer interviewing visitors to Skye! The Epsom and the Gerrards Cross cousins used to meet quite often. Kirsteen and David were full of fun; and on one occasion I heard laughing, as Kirsteen gave the usual greeting, "Shall we do a mischief, David?" Spending time with my four grandchildren has given me great happiness.

John, who has a good voice, used to sing Kirsteen and then Sally to sleep every night. It soon became evident that Kirsteen was musical but, after she had completed primary school, her parents decided not to enter her for a music school. In 1979 the family moved to Brecon in Wales. John had been appointed assistant head at Brecon College, and he was also a house-master. They lived in a large flat in one of the school boarding houses. We were all there for their first Christmas. It was the first time I had slept in a boys' dormitory! There were many advantages: we could use the school swimming pool, and we could use the splendid Sports Hall. I had just got bi-focals, and agreed to play a game of badminton. I was mortified to find that I had lost the skill — I kept missing the ball, and decided that I had suddenly become old.

It was a great relief when I discovered that you don't play such games wearing bi-focals. We walked on the Brecon Beacons but it was bitterly cold. Summer at Brecon was a joy; we walked beside what we had called in winter 'the wild roaring Usk', but now tamed, and we saw kingfishers. We read books about Wales and explored all the places mentioned in the popular books by Revd Francis Kilvert.

The girls enjoyed school at Brecon, but there was to be another move, this time in January 1986 to Scotland. John became Deputy Rector at Glasgow Academy, a day school, and Susan a senior social worker in child care. They bought a flat with a garden in Bearsden, across the road from Bearsden South Church. They both became elders of this church. Kirsteen went to Epsom College as a boarder and Sally to a local school. Susan and John spent a lot of time gardening with splendid results. They had to sell their Skye house at Roag to buy the Glasgow home, but managed to have their usual holidays in Skye. Time passed and Kirsteen went to Edinburgh University where she got a first-class honours degree in Music, and a scholarship for a year in Paris. When she was at Edinburgh, towards the end of her last year, she and five others decided to put on a show at the Edinburgh Festival Fringe – a lunchtime concert for six pianos. An agent showed interest in them and they formed a group, *Piano Circus*. At Christmas and Easter they made recordings for two albums with Decca. After Kirsteen's year abroad she settled in London, and for thirteen years was a member, and for a time organiser, of *Piano Circus*. The group performed at the Edinburgh Festival, New York, Istanbul, in Sweden, Portugal, Canada, the Scottish Highlands and Islands and elsewhere. *Piano Circus* continues but Kirsteen is now a member of another group.

When Sally left school she went to Edinburgh University and got a First in Italian. After travels in India and China she went to a college in London where she did a course in furniture design. She excelled in this skill, and has had some good commissions.

Few families continue successfully and happily without some

tragedies. By Christmas 1964 John and Audrey's boys had left school. Kenneth was at the Glasgow Vet School, Russell at St Andrews University; Lois was still at school in Milngavie. Susan was doing charity work, and after Christmas went as a volunteer to be cook at a hostel at Glencoe. She had just received the exciting news that she had been accepted to train for the police force. I woke up on 21st February 1965 and switched on the radio for the news. I heard that Susan Anderson of Milngavie was missing on the slopes of Glencoe, and search parties were out. When I rang up Barnellan Russell answered the phone. "Yes", he said, "Mum and Dad have been home for a few hours sleep and have gone back again to join the search party." Later in the day the worst news came through. Susan had been walking the dog of a local farmer, had slipped on an icy path down to a ravine and was dead. A cruel fate for a girl who had high ideals and who had done so much for other people in her brief life.

We have been a fortunate family in that we have had good health and been able to work hard, play hard, enjoy holidays in Scotland and abroad. Each year the Walkers and the Davidson Kellys took turns to invite us all for Christmas. In 1994 we were at Penny and John's. In June 1995 Susan rang me up to say she had bad news. She had not been well, had had some tests, and had just seen the specialist. She had a secondary cancer of the lungs and it had spread; he was not very hopeful of a recovery. She and John were determined to put up a good fight. She did well for some time. She was head of a team of child care workers, but was faced with having to retire. However she was asked to work part-time and to attend their frequent meetings, so she continued to do this. She was able to drive her car, and she met a different friend or friends almost each day. She said that one good thing was that she had never known she had so many kind friends. She did not want any fuss, nor the routine altered. She was her courageous cheerful self. She went into a hospice on 18 November, and died on 23rd November. She was fifty-four and had done so many good things in her too short life. She has been and is yet greatly missed, and I am sad to think of all *she* has missed, especially her daughters' weddings, and the babies, her grandchildren, who followed.

John D.K. heard of a house in Skye which was up for sale. It is at Ardroag, down by the water and with a view of the Cuillins. He bought it and when he retired from the Academy he was able to make frequent visits to Skye. Sally became engaged to Luke Francis, son of friends of John and Susan from Brecon days. We were all invited to the wedding, to be held at John's house at Ardroag. Kirsteen organised a willing work party, who decorated the village hall at Dunvegan ready for the reception. They gathered dozens of wild daffodils, and each table was decorated with candles and with bunches of little wild Skye daffodils placed in jam jars half filled with shingle from the shore. Everything was ready by the time we all assembled in the garden at Ardroag. John's brother, Tom Davidson Kelly, at that time the Minister of Govan Old Parish Church, took the service. And of course John D.K. played wonderful Scots tunes on the pipes.

A year later we had invitations from John D.K. to the wedding of Kirsteen and Bertie Fritsch. Kirsteen and Bertie had met in London through their work. Bertie is a sound engineer and a drummer. The wedding was arranged on the same lines as Sally's. One difference was a surprise. We were all waiting in the garden expecting Kirsteen to come out from the house, when a boat appeared; it was heading for the rocks in front of the garden. As it got nearer we saw it was the bride and bridegroom! John piped them to their places in front of Tom. The morning after the wedding John was piping again at the Dunvegan Castle pier, where almost everyone except me went into the cold, cold water for the traditional swim, much to the amazement of some Japanese tourists.

These were two happy occasions, and I was so fortunate to be there. Bertie and Kirsteen had found a converted studio in a secluded backwater in Hackney, and before long Sal and Luke bought the house next door but one. Luke was a master at Highgate School, and all four were working hard. From these families I soon had two great-granddaughters; they were Eloise Fritsch and Josie Francis. From the time they were babies they rejoiced in being together. One day Kirsteen took them in the double pushchair to the supermarket. As she went round she noticed a woman following her. Presently the woman came up, had a good look at the children and said, "Are they twins then?" "No" Kirsteen replied, "there is a month between them." The woman looked puzzled, then said, "However did you manage that?" Eloise and Josie were taken for walks together, played in the yard in front of their houses, visited each other homes, and went to nursery school together. A baby sister for Josie, Lola, was born in April 2002. Eloise was very interested, especially in Sally's method of feeding the new baby. At Easter time I was on a visit to Elgin and bought a baby doll which could be bottle fed, and sent it to Eloise. 'Baby Doll' went everywhere with her. I had a letter from Kirsteen in Skye to say that while they were on a walk they had come on a farmer's wife feeding lambs from a bottle. Eloise was delighted to be given a turn. Kirsteen wrote, "Eloise is an expert on both breast and bottle feeding."

Recently some big changes took place. Luke was appointed assistant head at Wakefield Grammar School in Yorkshire. Josie and Eloise were told about the move. It was hard for Eloise to believe that the Francis family was going to live in a strange house in an unknown place.

In July 2003, Kirsteen and family came to stay with me on their way to Skye. Not long before, they had been to the Cotswolds for a weekend, as Kirsteen was playing in a charity concert. When they came home they found that the house had been burgled. Their computers with all the musical records, and even the backups – five years work – had been stolen. Eloise said in a stern-teacher voice, "They have made a mess and they must come back and tidy it all up. If they do we will have them for tea." Next day when Kirsteen went to collect Eloise from nursery school the teacher said to her, "We wonder what has happened? Eloise said to us 'The Burghers came to our house and Daddy was shouting and Mummy was crying'."

When Kirsteen was on a course the next week, Bertie spent a lot of time looking after Eloise, seeing the police and dealing with the insurance. Then one day he went off to College on his byke. On the way back, cycling by the canal, two youths attempted to lassoo him. They were unsuccessful but charged him, knocked him off his byke and ran away with it. He was lying on the ground; his arm was broken and his back badly bruised.

When they got to St Andrews their wish and their aim was to move from London. Bertie had been applying for jobs. We had a lovely peaceful afternoon in Elie. When they were in Skye they had a call from the Gracefield Arts Centre at Dumfries to ask if he would come for an interview. This he did on their way home and he was offered the job, to be in charge of the Performing Arts. It seemed to be accomplished so quickly. At New Abbey they found a large house for rent and very soon they were settled there, Baby Doll and all. The baby Kirsteen was expecting was born on 14 November 2003 – of course it was a little girl. Her name is Zhara. I first met her at her grandfather John's house in Bearsden. Eloise asked if we would like her 'to do a show'. We sat round the room with a large space in the centre. Eloise is tall and slim, and wears what she calls twirly dresses so that she can dance. She went to the player to switch on the tape which had been made for her. She paused and said "Please do not clap and please do not tap your feet." We sat very still and she danced beautifully. At one point my foot tapped, and she danced over and pointed to it! I hastily sat quite motionless. The music changed to something slow and sad, and the dancer echoed this. When it came to an end, she said quietly "I am a sad, sad girl, far from home." It was very moving. However the cousins have seen each other as often as possible, and relatives and friends have been to stay at New Abbey, and the family are happily settled there.

I was over at Glasgow recently staying with John and Audrey. The Francis family were on a visit to John D.K's and Sal brought Josie and Lola to tea. Sal looked well and beautiful. They have found a suitable house near Luke's school and are buying it. Audrey had taken out the old toy farmyard – painted lead animals, fences, sheds and farm workers. Josie is a very industrious little girl and set to work to lay it out. Each collection of miniature sheep, cows, pigs, horses, poultry, etc. was placed in its own field. Lola was helping and occasionally knocked an animal over. I was struck with how kind and understanding Josie was. Eventually Lola worked with her own field and pile of animals; she put them all lying down asleep, an easier manipulation for her. Lola showed a liking for my brother John, and Sal told us that Lola 'prefers older men' – Luke's father, and especially her piper grandfather John D.K. When he has been to stay and has left, she cries sadly, "John – John – John".

Before they were married, Liz and Andrew Kelly had moved from Bristol to Cheltenham temporarily, as halfway between their two jobs. We were all delighted when Bethan Rose was born there in November 2002. The next spring they found lovely house in a little village near Malmesbury, Wiltshire. I saw Bethan in the summer when we all had an outing to the arboretum at Westonbirt. She enlivened our walk round this wonderful place with her eager interest, and she took a liking to the hydrangeas.

Bethan is now a very active and talkative toddler. She is a joyful little girl with a strong sense of fun. Sometimes she looks like a little imp. I was at Penny and John's this last Christmas (2003) and Liz, Andrew and Bethan, aged 14 months, were there. On Boxing Day my sister and John Huntridge came for lunch. We were standing round in the middle of the room talking and laughing. Bethan studied us and then, with her hands clasped behind her back she walked deliberately round the outside of the circle, imitating our laughter by a succession of loud HO HO HO HOs ! Penny tells me that Bethan now insists on getting out of her push-chair, and not walking – she *runs*.

This is almost the end of a family story of one line of descent, incidents from eight generations from 1806 down to 2004, dwelling mainly on the female side. Here is the line going from the past, from Elizabeth Smith to Bethan Kelly and my four other great-granddaughters who comprise our future.

ELIZABETH b.1763, oldest child of Barbara Gordon and Charles Smith

KETURAH GERARD b.1832, fifth child of Eliza Smith and Peter Merson

KETURAH b.1851, oldest child of Keturah Merson and Alexander Russell

MARY GORDON b.1884, oldest child of Keturah Russell and William Gordon Adam

ELIZABETH CAMERON b. 1915, oldest child of Mary and Will Anderson

ANNE PENELOPE b.1939, oldest child of Elizabeth Anderson and Rex Willsher

JANET ELIZABETH b.1965, oldest child of Penelope Willsher and John Walker

BETHAN ROSE b. 2002, oldest child of Janet Walker and Andrew Kelly

Time present and time past
Are both perhaps present in time future,
And time future contained in time past.
T.S. Eliot, 'In Burnt Norton'

The latest generations of those in the family with the name Keturah

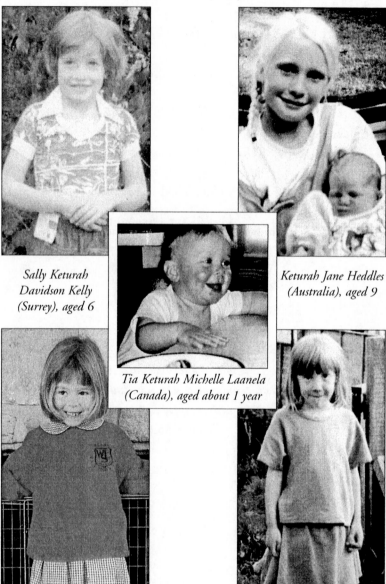

Sally Keturah Davidson Kelly (Surrey), aged 6

Keturah Jane Heddles (Australia), aged 9

Tia Keturah Michelle Laanela (Canada), aged about 1 year

Keturah Ann Adam (Elgin), aged 6

Katherine Keturah Ings (London), aged about 7

Four generations: Liz Kelly, Betty Willsher with Bethan Kelly and Penny Walker

New generations: Jack and Charlie Huntridge Dixon with Amanda

The author's five great-granddaughters

Josie and Lola Francis

Bethan Rose Kelly,

Eloise and Zhara Fritsch

APPENDIX

The search for the identity of Alexander Russell of Lyne and Peebles, born 1721

This may be a cautionary tale to keen amateur genealogists, such as I am. Among the papers left to me by my mother concerning her search of the Russell family, I have a copy of the inscription page of Thomas Russell's family Bible. [I quote only the first two lines.]

"My father Alexander Russell was born on 24 September 1721 and died 24 February 1774'

'I, Thomas Russell his eldest son was born 8th August 1751"

There follows a list of the children of this Thomas Russell, as in Chart B.

Members of this family of Russell in Peebles later gave the following information to my grandmother and my mother: Alexander Russell was related to the William Russell who founded Ashiestiel (on the river Tweed). As a young man Alexander held lands in the parish of Stobo, but these were confiscated after the '45 rebellion. He trained as a wright and he set up a business in the parish of Meggat and Lyne. Later he moved the business to Peebles.

My mother and granny called on the Misses Lockharts at Ashiestiel who said that they recalled that some years ago two Russell ladies from Peebles, probably daughters of Thomas(?) had been to see them and had claimed kinship from Alexander youngest son of the founder. Their reply had been that they did not think they could be of the direct line; they thought that William Russell's youngest son, Alexander, had been drowned when his children were quite young. They suggested this Peebles family might be from a cadet line in Stobo.

Many years later I myself went to see Colonel and Mrs Abel Smith at

Ashiestiel and was warmly welcomed. They took me to see the private graveyard in the grounds. But only the succession of heirs was recorded on the gravestones. I find the following in my notes: "The Ashiestiel Russells came from a well-to-do farming family in the parish of Stobo. There is a handsome mural monument to them on the outside wall of the east end of the church and it was erected by their 3 sons and 4 daughters. It is to James, who died 30th August 1692 and his wife Helaine Scott. (This James was a son of James Russ in Dreva.) James and Helaine's son William (1671-1746) bought Ashiestiel in 1712.'

I spent some weeks charting the descendants of these Stobo Russells, some of whom became professional men, some of whom were farmers. Subsequently it took me many weeks to research and make up a chart of the Ashiestiel Russells (parish of Yarrow). It *did* seem that William Russell and his wife had a number of boys. The youngest son *was* an Alexander; and I found that he married a Christian Bruntain at Traquhair; they had one son, William in 1740. Here I lost track and gave up for the time being. Some time later I was looking at the Yarrow OPR (the real live ones in the old register books!), and I came upon a block entry of the baptisms of the children of Alexander Russell of Elibank and his wife Christian Ballantyne – spelt Bannatyne at one point. The childen were James 1742, Samuel 1743, John 1747, Isabel 1748 and Robert 1750. The witnesses were William of Ashiestiel and/or his heir James. There was an entry written sideways in the margin, which looked as if it had been made later on. It was almost indecipherable. However, I had help. We agreed that it was "Thomas son to Mr Alexander Russell of Elibank and his wife Christian Ballantyne bap. 8 August 1751". So here it was! I was so elated that by the time I got to Leuchars Junction you might have thought I had been celebrating on the train with a bottle of champagne

Can you spot what was wrong with the Thomas entry I found in the Yarrow register? First the date of the birth in Thomas's Bible entry, which would surely be right, was a good month after the baptismal entry in the OPR. BUT the entry in the OPR was a later insertion and there *might* have been a mistake. Secondly Thomas stated he was the oldest son, but from the Yarrow records he was certainly not. Was he the oldest son of his father's third marriage?? Thomas was the name of Christian Ballantyne's father. Thirdly it was strange that none of the children listed in the Bible had been named Christian.

I will now tell you of the final crash of my hopes and confirmation of my doubts. A man who lives in Edinburgh had been told to get in touch with me, as he wanted to know if I had any information about a William Russell, son of Alexander Russell, son of William of Ashiestiel. I was able to give him the name of an old book called *Four Scottish Authors* by David Irvine; one section is on that William Russell. In return, my correspondent said he would look out for anything, which might be a clue to solving my problem. In due course a note came. He had been working at West Register House and come across the following in the Elibank papers (GD32/26/37), dated 28 November 1754.

> Memorandum for Mr Hew Crawford to be pleased to acquaint Lord Elibank that Mistres Russell in Elibank does not owe above a year's rent, that in March or Aprille next it shall be paid up within half a year; and that as the lease is expired, if my Lord will be pleased to give a new lease for seven eight ten or twelve years, William Russell, depute commissary clerk in Edinburgh will oblige himself for the tack duty or rent and pay it pointedly at Edinburgh twice a year, that this may help to support a poor widow and nine fatherless children.

Some years ago I had a visit from Dot and Stu Wallace of Savannah, USA, and descendants of the Peebles Russells. A good correspondence followed. Stu and a cousin of his by marriage, Pat Gerity, put me on to entries in Meggat and Lyne and onto the right Alexander, father of Thomas. But don't think it has been straightforward from then. How many times have I seethed with anger because Thomas did not put his mother's name in the Bible list. And how I wish he had put their names on the family tombstone at Peebles.

The list of Alexander Russell's children from the Meggat and Lyne OPR is as follows:

1. Thomas Russell bapt. 28th May 1751 witness Adam Russell of Burnfoot
2. Elizabeth bapt. 26th March 1753 witness as above
3. Adam bapt. 17th June 1757
4. Joan bapt. 4th May 1759
5. Barbara bapt. 19th November 1760
6. Margaret bapt. 27th April 1763

So you might take it that Alexander's father was either Adam Russell or Thomas Russell (one would probably be the name of his wife's father). By the same custom, was Alexander's mother Elizabeth or Joan?

Three of Alexander's children married, had children and lived at Lyne for some years. They were Thomas Russell and Margaret Grieve, Adam Russell and Janet McLean and Joan Russell and John Brodie. The name Alexander was given to children in all three families, also the name Margaret.

Lyne parish register is incomplete from 1683 to 1725. As for Stobo parish, the records start in 1783 for births and marriages but no mothers' names are recorded until 1802. But after 1808 there are some loose pages of earlier records with 18 Russell baptisms between 1660 and 1708 records, out of order before 1783.

Genealogists, beware wrong trails and disappointments.

BIBLIOGRAPHY.

Bailey, Philippa. *History of the Moncoffer Russells*

Blacks Morayshire Directory, *1863*

Briggs, Asa. *Victorian People: A Reassessment of Person and Themes 1851–67,* 1965

Chambers, Robert. *History of the Rebellion 1745-1746.* Edinburgh, 1827

Chambers, Robert. *Memoir of Robert Chambers with Autobiographical Reminiscences of William Chambers.* Edinburgh, 1872

Chambers, William. *History of Peeblesshire.* Edinburgh, 1864

County Directory of Scotland, for 1872, 1875, 1878

Cramond, William. *Records of the Kirk Session of Elgin, 1584 –1779.* Elgin, 1897

Cramond, William. *Church of the Parish of Alves. Elgin*

Dunbar, E. *Documents relating to the Province of Moray.* Edinburgh, 1895

Edinburgh and Leith Post Office Directories

Ferguson, A.J.A., Prescott, D.T. & Robertson, F.A. *A History of Medicine in Sout-West Durham.* The South-West Durham Health Authority, 1989

Forsyth, Isaac. *Memoir of Isaac Forsyth of Elgin 1786-1859.* London, 1889

Gunn, C.B. *The Book of Stobo Church.* Peebles Press, 1907

Gunn, C.B. *The Book of the Cross Kirk of Peebles*

MacAndrew, I.F. *Memoirs of Isaac Forsyth of Elgin, Morayshire.* Kegan Paul, London, 1882

Macintosh, H.B. *Elgin Past and Present, A Guide and History.* Elgin, 1891

Murray, A.D. *Burgh Records of Peebles,* 1862

Paterson, James. *Scottish Surnames: A Contribution to Genealogy.* Edinburgh, 1866

Rampini, Charles. *A History of Moray and Nairn*. Edinburgh, 1897

Renwick, R. *Historical Notes on Peeblesshire Localities*

Russell, Alexander. *The Morayshire Register*. Elgin, 1843 & 1847

Shaw, Lachlan. *History of the Province of Moray*. Glasgow, 1892

Smiles, Samuel. *Self Help with Illustrations of Character and Conduct*. London, 1860

Watson, James. *Morayshire Described*

Watson, Nigel. *The Last Mill on the Esk*, 1987

Williamson, Alex. *Glimpses of Peebles and Forgotten Chapters in its History*. Selkirk, 1895

Young, A.E. *The Story of the Elgin Guildry Fund*. Elgin, 1937

Young, A.E. *Annals of Elgin 1850-1876*. Elgin, 1879

Layout: Stephen M.L. Young
                     latouveilhe@mac.com

Font: Adobe Garamond (11pt)

Copies of this book can be ordered via the Internet:

                     www.librario.com

or from:

                     Librario Publishing Ltd
                     Brough House
                     Milton Brodie
                     Kinloss
                     Moray IV36 2UA
                     Tel /Fax No 01343 850 617